Paleo
Southwe
Walking and Hiking

Sam Jeffrey

Publisher: Independent Publishing Network.
Publication date:
Author: Sam Jeffrey
Distributor: Amazon.com
ISBN: 978-1-80068-175-0

Copyright © 2021 Sam Jeffrey

All rights reserved. No part of this book may be reproduced in any form or by any electronic or mechanical means, including information storage and retrieval systems, without permission in writing from the publisher, except by reviewers, who may quote brief passages in a review.

To request permissions, contact the copyright owner at Sam-J-Harris@Outlook.com

Dedicated to

Denys Morton

Thanks to:

Beverly Bailey for editorial work, cups of tea, walking the walks and putting up with me throughout.

1. Contents

2. Introduction 3
3. Walks Table 5
4. Walk Locations Map 6
5. Paleochora 7
   - A. Paleochora Town Tour 7
   - B. Paleochora Millstone Quarry 10
   - C. Paleochora Aerials 12
   - D. Paleochora-Anidri 15
6. Drive/Taxi/Bus 21
   - E. Vlithias 21
   - F. Azogires Monastery and Caves 23
   - G. Azogires, Spaniakos Fort and the Cave of the 99 Holy Fathers 25
   - H. Krios, Three Beaches 28
   - I. Voutas to Karavopetra beach via the Ridge Tombs 31
   - J. Voutas Churches 33
   - K. Kandanos Churches and Ancient Tree 36
   - L. Kandanos Southern Hills 39
7. Drive 42
   - M. Milia 42
   - N. Milia from Koutsomatados 46
   - O. Sarakina Valleys 50
   - P. Topolia Gorge 53
8. Ferries 56
   - Q. Agia Roumeli Lower West Fort 56
   - R. Sougia Circular 58

	S.	Sougia, Polyphemos Cave (Adventurous)	60
	T.	Sougia, Polyphemos Cave	63
	U.	Sougia to Paleochora	67
	V.	Elefonisi	71
9.		Popular Linear Walks	73
		Buses and Ferries for the Gorges.	73
	W.	Agia Irini Gorge	74
	X.	Samaria Gorge	76
10.		Errors, Omissions, Corrections	79
11.		Grading	79
12.		Fence-Gates	79
13.		Maps	79
14.		Ferries	80
		Ferry warnings	80
		Ferry Routes	80
15.		Useful Links	81
		Ferries	81
		Bus	81
		Taxi	81
16.		Satellite navigation, GPS and GPX	81
17.		Safety and Liability	81
18.		Walks Table in order of distance	82

2. Introduction

The southwest corner of Crete is a beautiful, peaceful place to walk with dramatic landscapes peppered with traditional villages where you are assured of a warm welcome.

These walks take you from shady olive groves and tree-filled valleys to rugged rocky hills and high coastal paths with spectacular views.

If you want to walk in Crete, Paleochora is the ideal place to stay. It still retains its traditional laid-back charm whilst being a lively town with plenty of shops, bars and tavernas. The town first became popular with hippies in the 1970's and continues to welcome visitors from around the world, many of whom return year after year, such is the lure of this charming town.

Paleochora at night: roads closed to traffic; tables in the streets.

Paleochora is also the start point for many of the walks including those utilising the ferry service between smaller coastal villages to the east, whilst others require a short taxi or bus ride. There are also walks further afield for those that want to explore with a hire car.

The town is located on a narrow peninsula dominated by the ruins of a Venetian Fort and has miles of coastline with a sea-front promenade full of bars and restaurants, a long, sandy beach and smaller rocky and stony beaches.

This book's primary purpose is to provide clear directions for walks whilst based in Paelochora, but it also applies to the southwest of Crete in general. It aims to allow you to spend more time enjoying your walk and less time working out directions. It endeavours to provide clear information with location numbers in the text relating to the numbers on the maps.

All walks have been undertaken and recorded on GPS, which are available to use on smartphones (details in the GPS section) and dedicated GPS devices. The maps provided show the actual routes taken using the open street map (OSM) format. All paths used have been added to the OSM maps where they were missing, so that the maps can be viewed and navigated in any App using OSM format (most of them do).

All the walk information and descriptions are provided first in the book, for easy access. Other information that may be useful to you is contained after the walking descriptions at the back. IT IS IMPORTANT TO READ the Safety and Liability section at the end of the book (section 17) before going on a walk.

To help choose something that suits your expectations and capabilities a table is provided at the front of the book summarising the main walk information i.e. location, distance, ascent/descent. For ease of selection, the walks are organised by most likely transport types to the start or return. Directions are provided from Paelochora from these, with the aid of a map you can work out how to access the walks from other locations. The final walk section provides a couple of the most popular linear gorge walks that do not require much in the way of directions but are great 'classic' walks. There are excellent ferries that hop along the coast from Paleochora which allow you to turn a linear walk into a circular with the ferry either taking you to the start of the walk or bringing you home. A map of the ferry routes along the coast is provided in the ferries section 14.

A map showing the start point of all the walks is provided directly after the walk table to help the planning of walks. Links are provided at the very end of the book where the latest information on transport timetables and other useful information can be found.

I started going to Paleochora back in 2005 on a group holiday with two weeks of walks organised by the guide Denys Morton, to whom this book is dedicated, he has now sadly passed away. I was introduced to this magical place, seemingly unspoilt by modern, mainstream, commercial holiday companies. With the properties and business still being locally owned, it is hoped that the character of Paleochora remains long into the future for everyone to enjoy.

For me the walks and their locations in relation to each other were very much a mystery, but over the years, on many return visits with my partner and friends, I have come to some extent understand the location of the mountain and coastal villages that surround Paleochora and how to link them up with footpaths, ferries and roads. Although some walking information with colourful descriptions of the area and history is available locally, it tends to need 'route finding' skills. The discovery and serendipity are part of the beauty and excitement of walking. The chance finds, the discovery of a hidden church, a rock tomb, a mountaintop view, a restaurant or a village, a secluded beach. So my book mainly concentrates on walking directions so that you too can discover the people and landscapes, flora and fauna, history and heritage of southwest Crete.

With the arrival of handheld GPS and latterly smartphones it has become easy to record and share walking routes to the extent that I found that in 2019 I had more than enough material to produce a book. And as it happens, more time than usual over 2020/21 to put it all together. It was my original intention to produce simple pamphlets with maps and make the GPS routes available. However, I realised some people still like walk directions and descriptions, but this was a far greater undertaking and a few trips back to re-walk the routes were required to clarify some of the route directions.

Photos have been included where possible, albeit mainly from our mobile phones so please excuse the quality.

From the Milia walk overlooking Kissamos bay, Oct 2020

So I hope you enjoy this book and find it useful, it might even inspire you to visit Paleochora and southwest Crete if you haven't done so before. You will find the people very friendly and hospitable, beer and wine chilled at the end of your walk and a magical atmosphere unlike anywhere else.

3. Walks Table

Walk	Name	Distance		Ascent		Pg
		Miles	km	m	ft	
A	Paleochora Town Tour	3.4	5.5	156	512	7
B	Paleochora Millstone Quarry	2.2	3.5	49	161	10
C	Paleochora Aerials	4.8	7.6	356	1168	12
D	Paleochora-Anidri	5.5	8.9	333 or 440	1093 or 1444	15
E	Vlithias	2.5	4.0	214	702	21
F	Azogires Monastery and Caves	2.8	4.5	305	1001	23
G	Azogires Spaniakos Fort and the Cave of the 99 Holy Fathers	3.1	5.0	312	1023	25
H	Krios, Three Beaches	4.5	7.2	332	1090	28
I	Voutas to Karavopetra beach via the ridge tombs	6.2	10.0	194 -472	636 -1550	31
J	Voutas churches	6.4	10.3	452	1780	33
K	Kandanos Churches and Ancient Tree	4.9 or 6.6	7.9 or 10.6	282 or 327	925 or 1071	36
L	Kandanos Southern Hills	6.7	10.8	441	1447	39
M	Milia	6.0	9.7	461	1512	42
N	Milia from Koutsomatados	7.3	11.7	655	2150	46
O	Sarakina Valleys	9.9	14.4	520	1706	50
P	Topolia Gorge	10.7	17.2	696	2283	53
Q	Agia Roumeli Lower West Fort	2.8	4.4	291	955	56
R	Sougia Circular	3.7	6.0	287	942	58
S	Sougia, Polyphemos Cave Adventurous	6.4	10.3	520	1703	60
T	Sougia, Polyphemos Cave	9.7	15.6	680	2231	63
U	Sougia to Paleochora	10.2	16.4	554	1818	67
V	Elefonisi	7.0	11.3	257	843	71
W	Agia Irini Gorge	4.7 or 9.0	7.5 or 14.5	-500	-1640	74
X	Samaria Gorge	9.3	15.0	-1250	-4101	76

All walks are circular when including those with outward or return journeys on a ferry. The exceptions are walk 'I' which needs a taxi to the start, and 'W' & 'X' which are bus there and ferry back. Walk 'V' is best accomplished with a taxi and ferry return.

4. Walk Locations Map

5. Paleochora
A. Paleochora Town Tour

Distance	3.4 miles, 5.5 km.
Ascent	156m, 512 ft
How to Get There	Take the eastern coast road heading south until you reach Haris Studios.
Start Point	Haris Studios Café or any point on the route

Description
This short walking tour of the town is ideal if you are new to Paleochora, and, if taken in the evening, can be combined with seeing the sunset from the Venetian fort. From the stony beach to the vast sandy beach, from the sea-front promenade to the bustling 'crossroads' you can get a feel for the layout of the town. Whatever time of day you take this trip be sure to stop, have a drink and watch the world go by, marvelling at the local driving and parking skills. This is not a guide to the restaurants and bars, those mentioned are there for direction finding only not as recommendations, that's not to say there's anything wrong with them. The map identifies about 34 establishments for food and drink, but this is not all of them and it is not practical to review them here.

Walk Directions
1)   Starting from Haris' Studios/Waters Edge Café head north along the coast road towards the ferry jetty. The first of many restaurants appear, on the LH side and the jetty comes into sight.

2)   At the jetty, to your left are the ferry ticket offices, one each on the roads to the left and right of the Vakakis Family bakery. Continue past the Jetty along the east Beach Promenade (although there is no beach here) and the many restaurants to be found there.

3)   All along the promenade, looking north you will see great views of the famous Crocodile rock formation out to sea. At the end of the main promenade pavement follow the road first left and then right past the popular Chalikia Beach, known colloquially as the 'Stony Beach' for clear reasons. At the end of the beach is the Oriental Bay Restaurant and rooms. Enter the restaurant seating area and turn left down a path to LH side of the building through to the road behind and turn left along the road. Across the road, if you are interested, is the town cemetery with many impressive marble-clad tombstones.

4)   Continue down the road past balconied buildings and take the first RH turn just after passing the back of Maria's Restaurants on your left. On reaching the main road, turn left and you pass the bus station and ticket office on your left, it has more of the appearance of a Café than a bus station. Take the next right at a crossroads where there is a sign saying to the beach and points left (stony) and right (sandy).

5)   Just past the two-storey school building, the road comes to a junction with a road across on a bend. Take the RH turn which is a gravel road past the side of the school on the right. This area is handy for finding a parking spot when all others are taken. Keep walking down the road past some waste land on the left. Turn left down a gravel road in front of some villas with terracotta roofs. This leads to the west sandy beach. Head more or less straight, bearing right toward the back of some apartments down a gravel track.

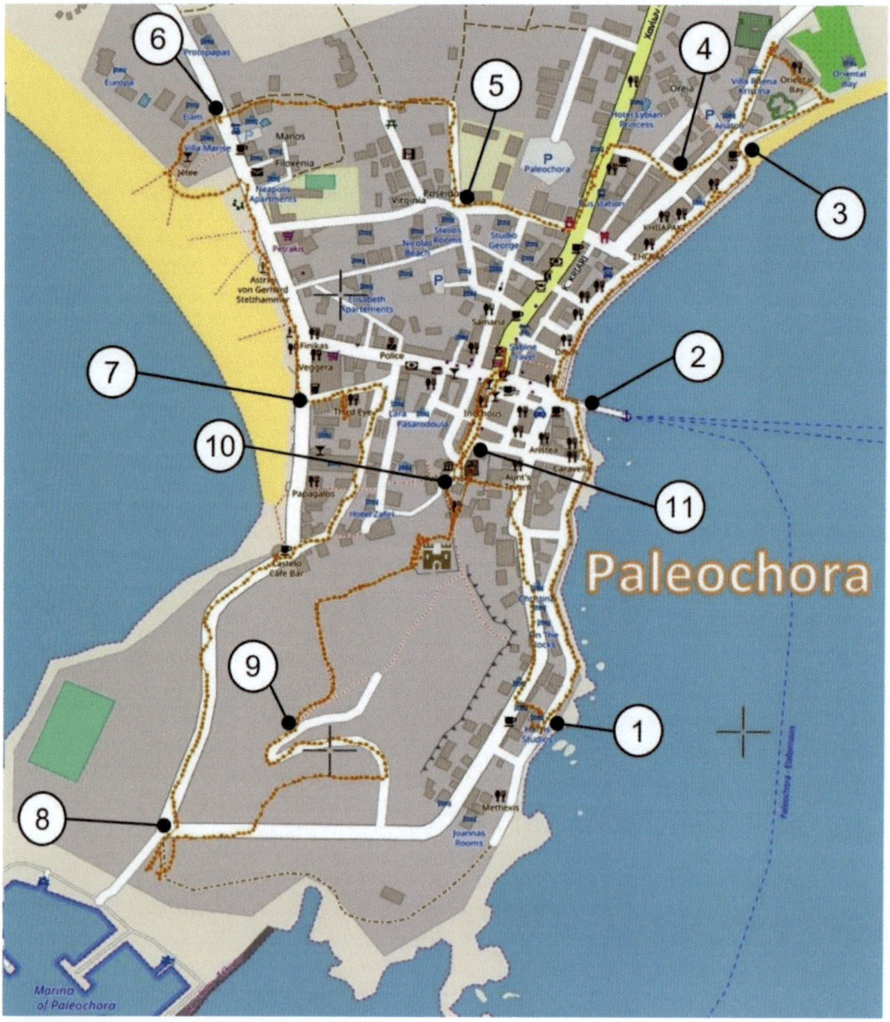

6) You should hit the road to the left of Notos car rentals and Relax apartments. Cross the road to the entrance directly opposite between a chain-link fence on the right and a stone wall on the left. This route leads you to the delightful Jetee bar with its tables under straw parasols. Walk around or through the bar and return to the main road. Then follow the road south along the side of the beach. You will pass a supermarket on your left and the "statue of a topless woman" (there must be a better name) on your right. You will come to the junction with the main road to your left up to the central crossroads. Don't take that but keep straight on passing the metal Travellers sculpture of two men and a donkey and an old ship's anchor on the right. Just past the main road junction is the

back entrance to the other main Paleochora supermarket. Keep straight on the coast road to the next LH turn.

7) Take this LH turn down the RH side of the Atoli restaurant, this will bring you to the Third Eye vegetarian restaurant on your RH side. Take the next RH turn just before a yellow concrete building and follow the road, eventually bearing right out onto the beach road opposite the Castello Café Bar overlooking the length of the beach. Turn left and follow the road to the port area with the fort walls above on the LH side. Look out for a rock formation that looks just like the head of a cow on the RH side and after it (possibly, as missing in Oct 2020) is an interesting large wood sculpture by Kostas Liatakis called Statue Anadysis.

8) At the end of the road follow it around to the left, you may wish to take a detour to view the port and the boats, look right amongst the trees on the other side of the road to see the kennels for stray dogs created by concerned residents. Just past some new villas on the left, turn left up the road signposted Enetic Castile Forteza and wind your way up to the fort plateau.

9) At the top take a path to the left which heads towards a modern building then take another LH fork which leads to the LH side of the fort ruins that is also known as the Fort of Selino. There are great views from the fort and the western wall is a popular spot to watch the sun set behind the hills towards Elephonissi. There is a new information board in the northeastern corner where you will also find the steps down into the town.

10) Take the steps down from the fort towards the church, passing a restaurant that looks out over the town. On reaching the church gates it is strongly suggested that you take the opportunity to walk past them to the main crossroads and explore all the shops, bars, restaurants and cafes and then, when finished, return to the church gates.

11) Enter the gates and cross the church plaza and exit via a gate in the top LH corner. When reaching the road turn right and

follow this road passing to the left of a restored stone house. Take the second left down the side of Haris' apartments to complete the route and arrive back to the start point.

B. Paleochora Millstone Quarry

Distance	2.2 miles, 3.5 km, total there and back
Ascent	49m, 161ft
How to Get There	Travel to the sandy beach on the west side of Paelochora
Start Point	Any point along the beach

Description
A very pleasant short walk, suitable for a mid-summer hot day or in the evening. Mainly along the shoreline to reach an interesting beach quarry, where millstones have been cut out of the flat rocks. These are estimated to date from Roman, Venetian and later times and similar sites can be found throughout the Mediterranean, but this is the only surviving quarry in Crete. Across the road, there are a couple of striking rock arches to see as well before you return.

Walk Directions
1)   Start by walking northeast along the 'Sandy Beach' towards the end that is away from the town. There is no obvious path, choose any route across the sand and stones that you prefer. Be aware that the far end of the beach is for nudists.

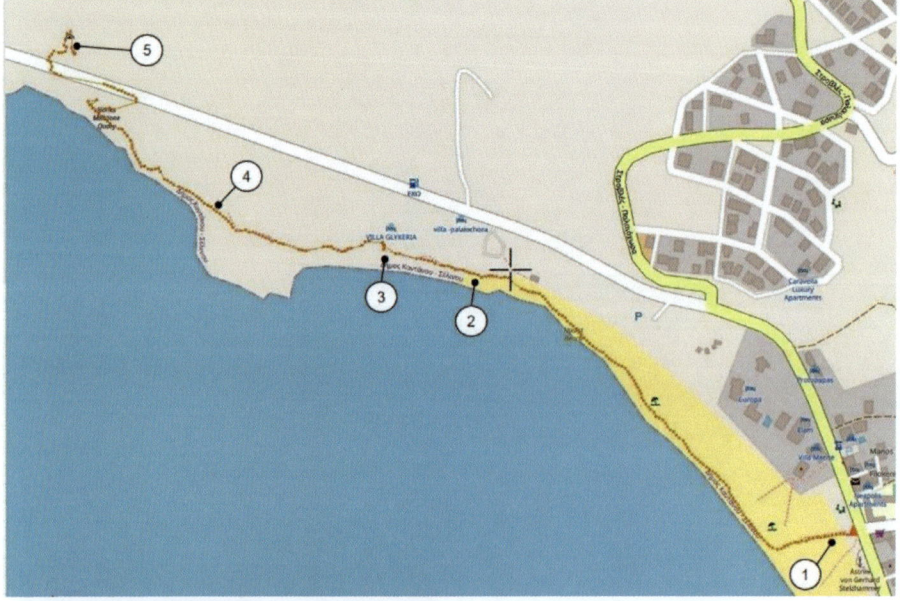

2)   Head past the last of the beach beds and shades, pass below the 'Tavern Limnaki Beach', an excellent bar/cafe in which to sit and watch the world go by. Keep going straight and take a route through the rocks on the shingle. There is no clear path, just follow the shoreline.

3)   You will come to a part where the trees and bushes come down to the waterline. To avoid getting your feet wet climb up to a wire fence and turn left into an open area. Go a short way out into

the open and then descend down again through some bushes to the shoreline, before reaching another wire fence. Continue along the shoreline and at an end of a bay climb up to more solid ground travelling straight on, missing out the rocks that jut out into the sea.

4) The ground flattens out and then descends again to a grey, sandy and stony beach. At the far end, there are flat rock surfaces, that are the quarry. Keep going and look around to see the many circular shallow holes revealed, where the millstones have been cut from the rock, possibly hundreds of years ago to grind cereal crops or maybe olives. You can't miss them they are everywhere, dozens of them.

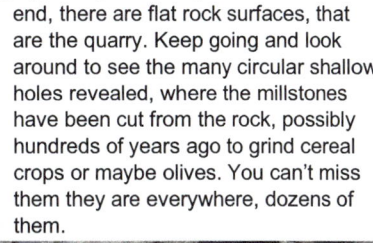

5) Across the road from the quarry, are a couple of impressive large natural stone arches

which are well worth going to explore. When finished, take the same route back along the shore or go back along the road which now has a new pavement (under construction at the time of writing).

C. Paleochora Aerials

Distance	4.8 miles, 7.6km
Ascent	356m, 1168ft
How to Get There	Paleochora
Start Point	Paleochora Sandy Beach (west side of peninsula) or join route anywhere from town.

Description
The aerials up on the hills behind Paleochora can be seen from anywhere in the town and if you fancy a good stretch of your legs with some great views this is a good walk that won't take too long. Rather than taking the obvious (but uninteresting) way up the service road, this route approaches the hills from the east and offers a slightly more adventurous route that loops back to the town. From the top, the best panoramic views of the town can be found and it is surprisingly peaceful.

Walk Directions
1)   Starting at the road along the sandy beach, walk south with the beach on your RH side.

2)   Turn left at the Palm Tree Restaurant onto the main road across town. Pass through the main town crossroads keeping straight on until reaching the ferry port at the other side of the peninsular.

3)   Turn left at the ferry port and walk up the promenade with the sea on your right, keep on this road until the very end, where it curves around to the left.

4)   Follow the road around to the left so that the 'stony' beach is on your right. On meeting the road going across in front of you with a blue road sign pointing left to Chania and left to Anidri (in Greek). Take the road right to Anidri passing the town cemetery on the left. Stay on this road.

5)   After a sharp RH turn, you will approach a bridge with metal railings. Take the gravel path left immediately before the bridge. (the map shows taking the path just after the bridge and then turning left to join the first path). Keep following this path past the houses and buildings as it gets narrower.

6) Turn left between these buildings

6) The path turns left, through the buildings and then right, going up steps, it is marked with orange paint. Walk along a narrow concrete path between a wall to the left and a fence to the right.

7) Keep following the orange paint to find a large pipe crossing the path. Duck under the pipe and the path joins a concrete road that takes you up to the main road.

8)   On reaching the main road look left to see on the other side of the road a stony earth hillside with olive trees before a formation of large grey rocks. Looking for the steep rough earth path up from the road starting just before the rocks and passing to the right a large rusty pipe poking out of the hillside.

9)   Cross and head left down the road and take a RH path up the hillside initially heading back in the direction you have just come. The path zig-zags up the hillside steep at first but eventually becoming a gentle ascent following the route of a wire fence on the left.

First set of aerials

10) After about 200m the orange dots start to lead around to the right and more steeply up the hill. Up ahead look for the outcrops of rock that are to be climbed. It may look difficult from here but is not as intimidating as it appears. Keep following the route upwards and to reach the crest with a clear route to the first set of aerials.

11) There are good views from the aerials, and it is a natural resting point. From here to carry onto the next aerial station, follow the road down and across the dip between the two aerial stations.

12) On arriving at a turning left carry straight on, that is the return route back to town. The road now zig-zags up to the second set of aerials and it is not beyond invention to take shortcuts should you choose.

13)   Enjoy the views from the second Arial station by venturing a little further on and towards the edge, you can arguably get the best most full views of Paleochora from here. To continue, make your way back down the road turning right at point 12 on the map and follow the concrete road down.

View of Paleochora in its entirety from the second set of aerials

14)   On a steep descent the orange dotted route takes a short cut off the road avoiding the corner below. There is option to stay on the firmer road surface to end up in the same place.

15)   On reaching the road at the Panorama apartment buildings, carry straight on, down the eastern outskirt road.

16)   At the end of the road where it turns right carry straight on using a small path to the road below. Cross to the other side of this road and follow it left a short distance to a LH bend. On the apex of this

bend, there is a path leaving the road down to the right, hard to see until you are actually upon it. Take this rough gravel path zig-zagging down.

17) Pass a church almost hidden amongst the trees on the left as you descend. The path straightens out to pass between a wall on the left and a fence on the right.

18) Carry on reaching a T junction with a gravel road going across in front of you. Turn right to reach another junction and turn right again. Keep on this large gravel road as it turns left to eventually reach the main road and turn left to reach the starting point.

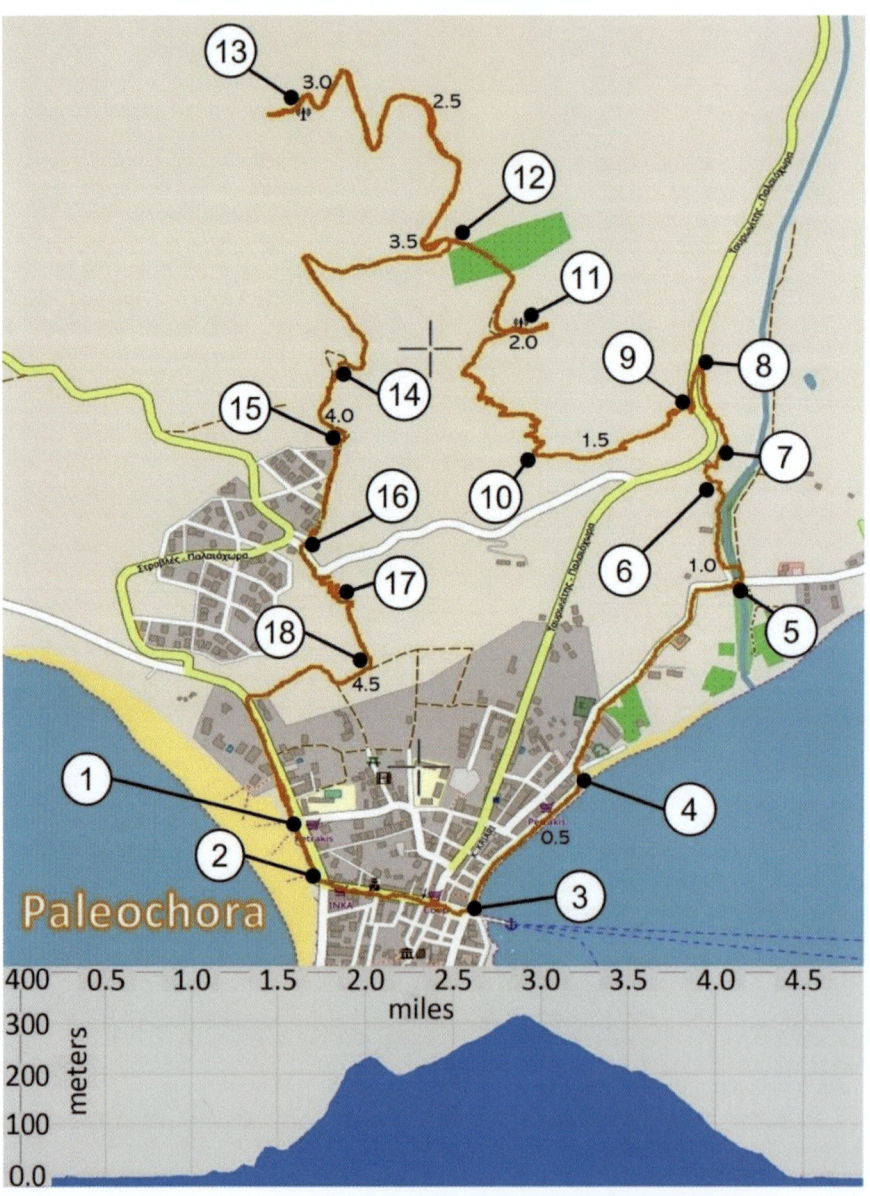

D. Paleochora-Anidri

Distance	Green route 5.54 miles, 8.9km. Green route with Orange detour 6 miles, 9.7km. Add 2.2 miles, 3.5km to start from and return to centre of Paleochora.
Ascent	Green route 209m, 686ft Green route with Orange detour 374m 1227ft
How to Get There	Car, taxi, or walk from Paleochora (1.2 miles from centre crossroads). Take the southeast (ferry side) coast road past all the restaurants. At the end, the road curves around to the left to a junction, turn right for the road to Anidri beach. Follow the road through the olive groves and pass Paleochora Camping on the left. Just after a 90 degree LH bend take a right fork heading steeply down to RH bend and a bridge. Just after the bridge is a LH turn to Olive Tree Cottages, this is the start point. There is some parking available at the start point and by the bridge.
Start Point	The turning to Olive Tree cottages from the main track to Anidri beach.

Description

Walking to Andri and enjoying the excellent local, unusual and creative cuisine to be found at the Old School House is arguably one of the best-known walks from Paelochora. Turning it into a circular walk which involves a lunch stop, an interesting descent via the Andri gorge and a stop at the beach for a rest and a swim makes it an enjoyable full day. Above Andri is the small church of the Prophet Elias, perched on a steep pinnacle of a hill with spectacular views which can be added in as an optional route along with another hill if you are feeling energetic. This is a favourite walk of ours and never fails to delight.

Two Routes

There are two routes shown on the map:

- Green route:- encompasses the entire walk but avoids the ascent of two hills between the start and Anidri. This is the easier of the two routes.
- Orange route:- is a detour from the green route that takes in the two hills. The first has good views back to Paleochora the second is a charismatic peak topped by the Church of the Prophet Elias.

Green route

5) Orange route: take path right, to leave the track

1) Start by taking the side road up to Olive Tree Cottages and immediately look for a rough track on the right-hand side of the bank to a wire gate with the route marked by orange dots.

2) The path follows the direction of the road below initially and is narrow, it turns steeply right heading up the hill, stay with the path and to pass some aerials on the right.

3) Keep following the orange dots and climb the hillside, zig-zagging back and forth with great views back to Paleochora.

4) After climbing up and passing through a fence-gate follow the path right which becomes a wider gravel track.

5) The route now levels off and after a slow curve to the left. To take the Orange route on the map look for where orange way marked route turns off the main

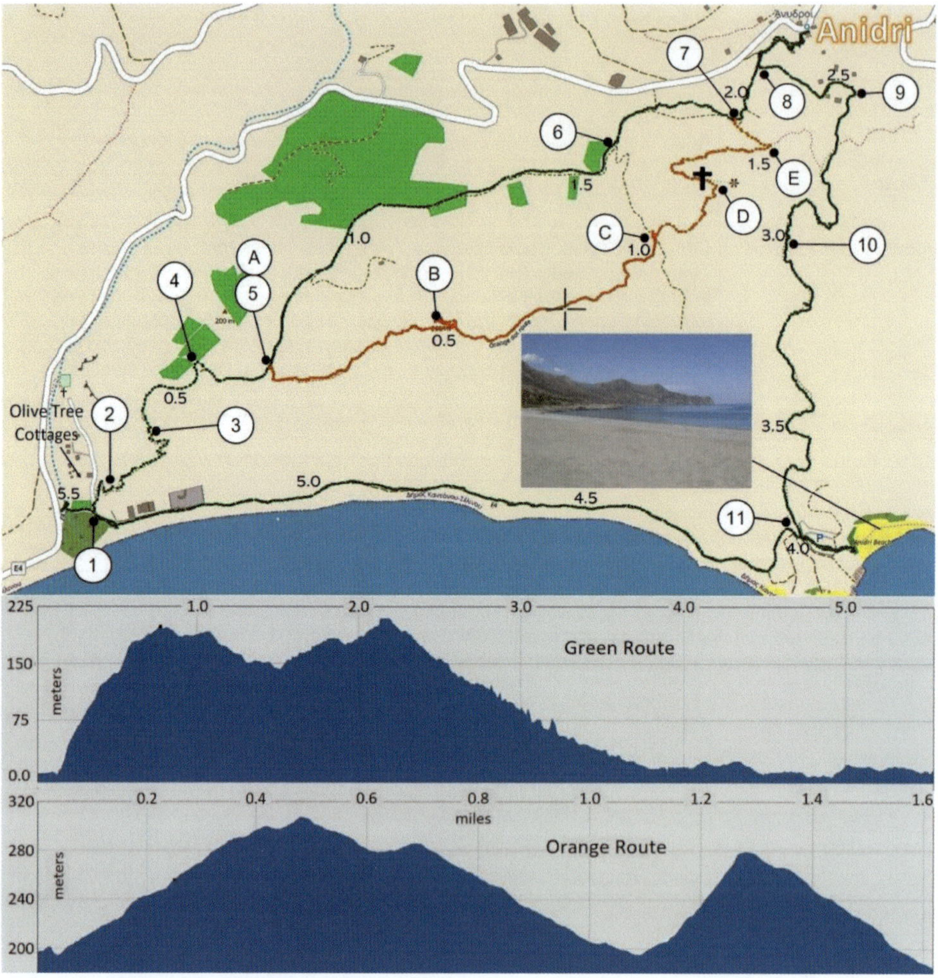

track to the right under a tree (pictured), use the directions starting para. A page 19. To continue on the Green route, carry straight on, i.e. remain with the main gravel track.

6) Now simply keep following the main gravel track downhill until you eventually come to a large outcrop of rock in front of you at the base of the hill on the RH side of the track. There is a sharp turning right up a steep track which goes to the start of the path to the church. Do not take this but continue straight on. Follow the track as it curves right until a left-hand bend is reached. Going left heads up to the main road to Anidri, this is an option should you wish to shortcut the route to the restaurant along the road. Just after the LH bend, there is route through the fence on the RH side marked with red dots. Pass through the fence to join a vague path to the right of a gully which is on the right of a fence going the same direction. Take the path and head east. It

Route through fence marked with red dots

must be admitted that the route is a little vague here not because there is no path but because there are too many options. If available it's best to keep to the GPS route. In general you need to keep heading east passing through fence-gates where you find them until you reach the route that crosses north south from Anidri to the church on the hill. Keep heading east running roughly parallel with the road above on the left. Look for a fence-gate that is between two trees. Pass through the fence and keep straight on. Next pass through a fence-gate to the right of a tree roughly in the middle of the fence. Move towards the RH terrace and climb up on it just in front of a large rock marked with red painted arrow. Walk along the edge of the terrace and pass through another fence-gate behind a tree with red paint on a rock to the side of it. The route now passes through an opening in a fence with no gate. Keep going straight ahead (east) and find some orange markers of a route crossing your path, this is the route to the church from Anidri. There is an orange marker on the fence to the left where there is a gate. Pass through the gate to join an avenue of olive trees heading towards Anidri, carry straight on.

Move up onto terrace in front of a large rock with a red arrow on it.

7)   The track starts to ascend past some fenced off inhabited land on the right, replete with very barky dogs (well for us anyway) that were free on the track but hid behind the fence as we passed. Pass the buildings up to the next junction.

8)   The route joins the corner of a concrete road, turn right and follow the "To The Beach" signs to find the gorge.

It is highly recommended that you detour to visit the Anidri School House Restaurant at this point. To do this turn left at the concrete road and then take the next right along a path to the church. Climb up

to the left of the church cemetery and pass the church to bring you out to an opening to the side of the restaurant terrace. Return the same way.

9) Following the concrete road downwards it funnels into a narrow path at the end with a tricky descent into the gorge itself. You cannot go wrong now, simply keep following the floor of the gorge downwards towards the sea. However, the going can be a little tricky through ancient water-eroded rocks and a little invention is required here and there to find the best route to take. That being said, there are clear orange markers and cairns for the most popular options.

10) A little bit of fun on the way is the "water-slide" which is a vertical rock descent of about 10' (~3m) with a body sized slide worn into it by the flowing water over immeasurable time. There is no water there now. Descending the side used to be fun, but some killjoys have installed a rope ladder and knotted rope to make it easy. Having completed this route with all sizes of people of all ages, I can say that with a bit of teamwork it never presented a problem. There is an alternative descent around to the left. Keep following the gorge path towards the coast road passing through a clear cleft in the valley with hills on either side. The coast is approaching when the occurrence of large rocks in the gorge starts to lessen replaced by small rocks under foot, then eventually gravel.

11) When you reach the gravel road crossing in front amongst scrub bushes there is a large car park to the left. The return route is right, heading west along the coast road.

Before turning right for Paleochora you could be easily excused of availing yourselves of the excellent beach, (correct name Gialiskari Beach) maybe taking a cooling swim and enjoying the food and drink available at the Imbiss Taverne beach bar, not to mention the free, hotel class toilets.

Seating in the shade at the Imbiss Taverne, Gialiskari Beach

12) The coast road return route is simple, heading west back to the start point. There are no direction decisions to be made. It's about a mile and a half of not too interesting well used gravel road. There is sometimes the opportunity to hitch a lift if there's not too many of you, in fact, we've been offered lifts before without even asking. People are good in this part of the world.

Orange Route

A.   Turn off right under a tree on the right of the main gravel track following the orange paint marked route. The initial path is a very sharp turn right almost doubling back at an acute angle. It is bordered initially with rows of stones. On reaching a fence-gate pass through it and turn left, heading east up the hill to the right of the fence. The route is clearly marked with dobs of orange paint. Keep heading up the hill directing towards the right of the rocky peak which comes into view up ahead

B.   As you approach the crest you will see a lone tree to the right just beyond the rocky peak, the path passes the peak and goes under the tree. This is a good resting place to admire the views, including the church on the hill up head which is the next destination for this Orange route. You can, should you choose, scramble up the rocks and get to the highest point, for even better views, it is not difficult. The peak is marked with a concrete pillar. The route continues to the right of the tree (coast side) and makes its way to the edge and around the hill side, again following the orange markers

View back to Paleochora from highest point on the hill

C.   Keep descending from the peak to eventually join a gravel track at an acute angle. Turn left along the track and then immediately right to cross the track where there are orange markers (pictured) and follow a path through some scrub land to the left of a fenced off area going towards the base of the hill. The route up to the church is marked with the usual orange paint. Follow the path climbing up and scouting around the south side of the hill. Although it may not look it at times the path is good to the top with great views down to the coast.

C) Path from track up to church

D. Approaching the top there are stones marking both sides of your route as the church comes into view at the summit. Take your time and enjoy the views from the summit reaping the fruits of your labour. There is a view point to the west where the entire length of gorge can be seen and the beach at the end. It is all downhill from here to the start of Anidri Gorge and then to the beach. The church is open should you wish to take a peek, please make sure the door is secured afterwards. To continue, the descent path is the opposite side of the church to the approach route, and behind the bell tower. Take this clear, well used path all the way to the bottom of the hill.

Prophet Elias Church

E. After the steepest part of the ascent is over the path doubles back on itself, be careful to catch this change in direction. As usual, keep following the orange markers. A little further on there is a fence-gate. Go through the gate descending to join a gravel track and turn right. You are now at point 7) page 17 of the Green route, follow those directions from here on.

6. Drive/Taxi/Bus
E. Vlithias

Distance	2.5 miles, 4 km
Ascent	214m, 702 ft
How to Get There	Drive out of Paleochora on the Chania Road to Vlithias 6.9 km. Or take the bus or a taxi. Pass the turning to Azogires on the right and then pass through Kalamos about 2.4 km later with concrete houses on either side of the road. After another km, you approach Vlithias, on a sharp RH turn with a concrete house on the right there is a small road off to the left which takes you into Vlithias. There is no parking there and the best start point is to remain on the main road and to park on the left where there is a layby and bus stop with more than enough room for additional cars.
Start Point	Layby on the west side of the main road next to Vlithias

Description
This is a nice short walk that allows you to explore the valley leading down to Paleochora which is only normally glimpsed from the main Chania road. Great views across and down the length of the valley towards Paleochora. At the bottom of the valley, stop at the river at the bridge, ideal for a game of Pooh sticks. This is a good walk for a hot day with plenty of shade from the trees and not too strenuous.

Walk Directions
1) Take the path at the centre of the layby down to a delightful well-kept village church and graveyard. It is the Church of the Transformation of the Saviour. Pass to the left of the church graveyard under a shelter and take the steps downwards to the road below. Across the road are the steps used on the return, we don't take them but turn right along the road behind the church.

2) Stay on the tarmac road until reaching a gravel track on the LH side which heads sharply backwards down the hill. Take this track.

3) Follow the track taking a RH turn down into the valley with the track going through a distinct cleft in the rocks. Here you can climb the RH side to find a stone threshing circle. Just after the cleft, there is a junction, turn right, down to a LH hairpin bend, follow the track around the bend. The track now becomes overgrown and indistinct but keep following it down to the river hidden amongst the trees.

4) Approaching the river, head right and look for a concrete dam where there is a crossing to the bank on the other side, cross the river and turn left.

5) Due to flooding, debris and erosion, this part of the walk on the other side of the river is most unclear. However, follow the river a short way until the loose stones end and it is hard to go any further with trees blocking the way on the riverbank. Here look for a narrow loose stone path on the right up the hillside through the bushes to the left of a gulley. Keep faith and go up the path climbing up and to the left to arrive out onto a proper gravel vehicle track. Turn left along the track

6) The route now is quite straight forward following the vehicle track around the contours of the valley through the olive groves with views across and down the length of the valley towards Paleochora. Ignore a RH turn up the hillside just after a RH bend and remain on the main track.

7) The track starts to descend around a series of zig-zags back down the valley to the river. Ignore the track off to the right on the first bend.

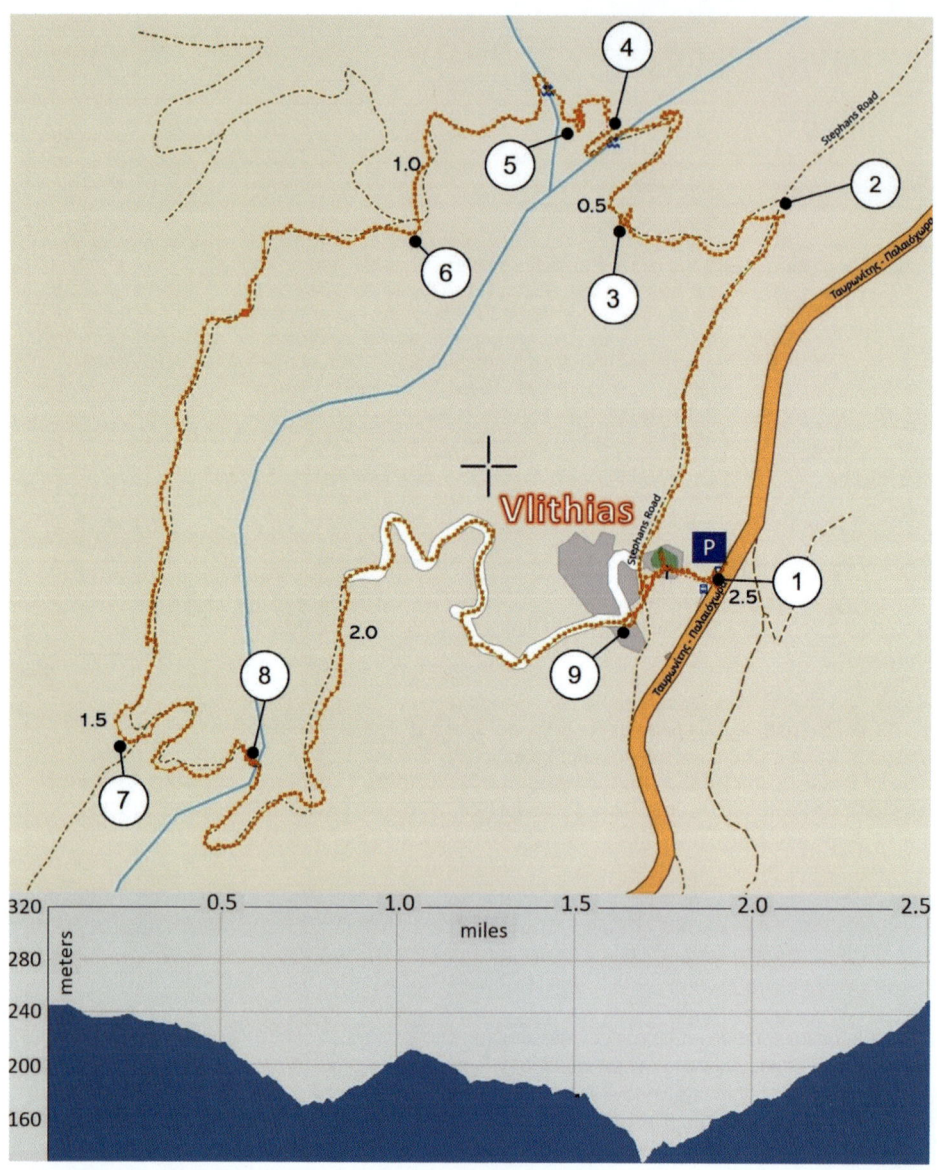

8) At the river is a rather delightful bridge and an excellent opportunity for competitive pooh-sticks. It is also a good place to stop in the shade of the trees. Cross the bridge and turn right climbing up the track and around a 180-degree bend climbing all the time. Keep on this track which eventually becomes concrete. Ignore side turnings off to houses and remain on the main road up to the village.

9) In the village, you will pass the old communal clothes washing baths on the left. Just afterwards there are steps up on the right to the road above which is below the church (marked as a path on the map but it is a road). Take the steps up to retrace your route back to the start point.

F. Azogires Monastery and Caves

Distance	2.8 miles, 4.5 km
Ascent	305m, 1001 ft
How to Get There	Drive, bus, or taxi to Azogires from Paleochora.
Start Point	The start point is the second wooden picket gate (the first gate is private) in a fence marked 'Path to Anidri Monastery' in a small layby on the RH side of the first LH bend as you leave the village heading north.

Description

This is a short but charming walk that introduces you to the ancient village of Azogires. On the walk discover the 99 Holy Fathers Monastery and museum, a beautiful Venetian bridge, an old schoolhouse and then up to explore some interesting carved caves which you can explore if you have a head for heights. When you return be sure to stop for a drink at the Alpha café and meet Lucky, who keeps the myths, legends and folklore stories of Azogires alive. Ask him about access to the museum.

Walk Directions

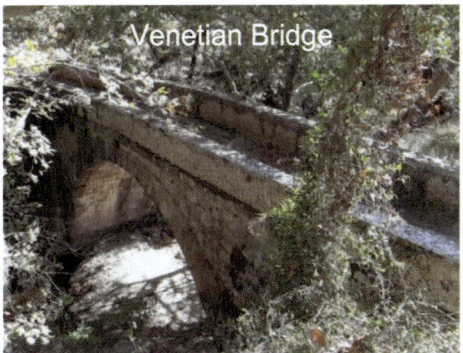
Venetian Bridge

1) Pass through the gate and go down the path between two buildings at the end of the buildings turn right and follow the path down towards the river. Optionally detour and turn left instead to view the waterfalls through the rocks and then return to the RH turn. Follow the path and after a short while, a stone Venetian bridge can be seen to the left slightly lower, crossing the river. Leave the path on arrival at a LH path taking you down to and across the bridge. At the other side of the bridge turn right along the path. On reaching another bridge on the left, carry straight on and pass some seating up to the Monastery of the Holy Fathers. After you have explored the Monastery carry on along the path past the front of it.

2) After a short while, the derelict large stone old schoolhouse appears. Our route passes in front of this building and then turns left up the side of it through a gate. This leads to a higher path through another gate in front of some goat shelters. Go through the gate and turn right and follow the path through the trees with blue markers.

3) The path becomes a gravel track and then a very wide gravel track at a junction where the track goes downwards to the right to Anidri and up to the left to the caves. Take the route up to the left. This route leads to the first caves joining with another gravel road from the left after a gate. Follow the track to the caves.

Steps cut into rock face

4) Some considerable effort has been made over the years to make the cave area presentable and improve the access to them. Known as the carved caves, the first lower cave is accessed by a wooden ladder. The second upper cave is accessed via steps cut into the rock face and improved with concrete. There is now a handrail as well as a rope pinned to the rock face to assist you. All the same, this climb will not be a favourite with those nervous of heights or Cretan levels of safety. Climb

at your own discretion this book cannot qualify the safety of climbing up to the caves. That being said it is well worth the effort and quite exciting should you choose to do so. Improvements have included a nice wooden bench in the cave and most of the goat droppings have been removed!

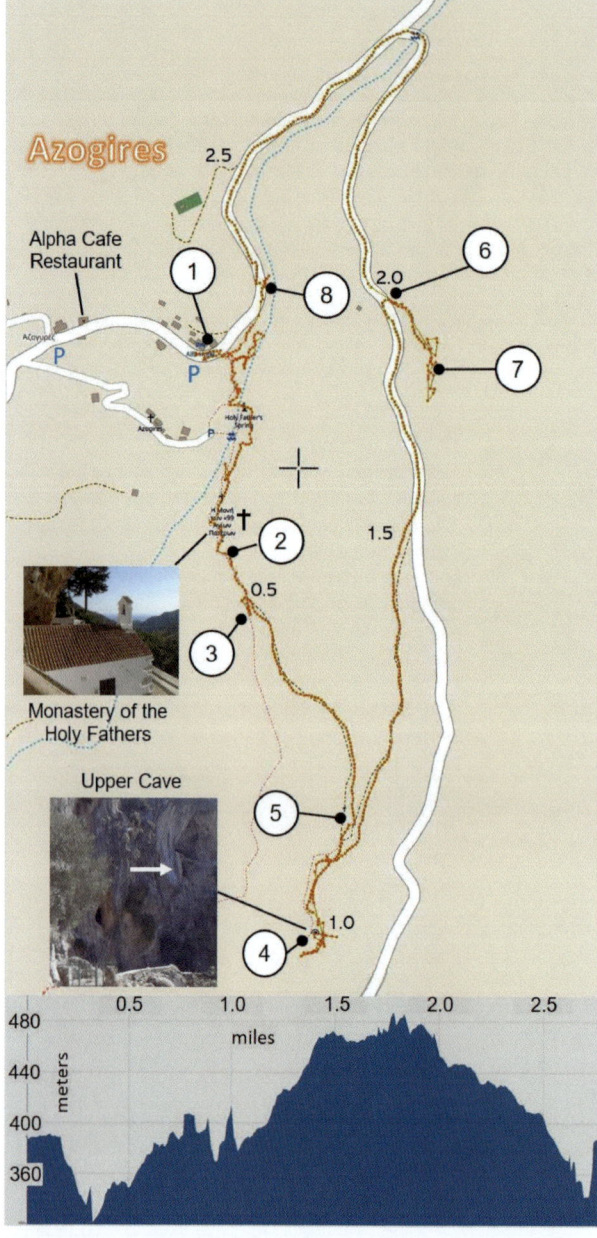

5) To continue the walk, return via the approached track to the caves and take the RH fork you merged with earlier. The track climbs 0.5 miles to the road above, at the road turn left.

6) Keep heading along the road and after 340m find the sign written in red paint saying 'Koukoutsakis caves' with a red arrow underneath pointing right. The sign is on a wire fence perpendicular to the road on the RH side. It is at the start of a gravel track heading up the hillside and is found just after the road reduces in width from the LH side. Taking the track, you are immediately greeted with a fence-gate. Head through the gate and take the path to the right through the trees. The route is marked with faint red dots.

7) Follow the path through the trees and approach a rocky hillside on the left, this is where the caves can be found. It is necessary to leave the path to go up to the caves which are dotted all along the rock face. There are 6 in total some easier to find than others. Some have written above the entrance in red paint 'Cave' with a number. Heading southwards the last one can be found up against a fence blocking further progress. After visiting the caves return to the road and turn right back to Azogires. At the end of the road after crossing the river is the junction with the main Azogires road, turn left here towards the village.

8) At the start of RH bend before you arrive back at the start point there is a gate on the LH side that leads down to the 'waterfalls'. These are quite quaint and worth the visit, the main one is to the left and there is a kiosk there which is sometimes open. To return to the start point follow the path along the side of the river to reach your original path up through the houses back to the start point layby.

G. Azogires, Spaniakos Fort and the Cave of the 99 Holy Fathers

Distance	3.1 miles, 5 km. Add 0.95 miles, 1.52 km from Azogires centre.
Ascent	312m, 1023 ft, Add 133m, 437ft from centre of village
How to Get There	Drive, bus or taxi to Azogires. Approaching into the village, there is a RH turn just after a RH bend. Between this turn and the first large concrete building on the left, there is a small stone building with a terracotta roof with a concrete road rising very steeply on its LH side. This is the road to the start point. Do not be put off by the initial steep ascent if your vehicle finds it difficult, it is less steep from then on. The alternative is to park in the village and walk-up. Keep up the road and its many hairpin bends until you arrive at a church on the LH side.
Start Point	The start point is by the church where the road is wide enough to park a few vehicles. If walking, there's no need to go to the church and you can start at the track to the left just before the 180 degree RH bend below the church.
Car Parking	On the LH side of the road by the church. This is not a dedicated parking spot but merely where there is room to park and not block the road. There is far more room to park at the top of the road where it meets the path that runs between the Fort and the Cave of 99 Holy Fathers. You will then need to walk down the road to the start point.

Description
An interesting walk, quite steep at times, with good views of Paleochora and the Libyan Sea and an old Fort to explore, but the highlight of the walk is the large Cave of the 99 Holy Fathers which is accessed by descending a series of ladders.

Walk Advise
Long trousers are recommended to pass through some of the sharp scrub bushes up to the fort. Bring a torch for the cave. The climb up to the Fort is a difficult very steep climb through bushes on loose ground, but not dangerous. It is recommended that you use GPS for navigation because the route gets lost amongst a myriad of goat tracks. If you don't fancy the climb, you can drive to the top and visit the Fort and Cave from there rather than do the walk.

Walk Directions
1) Walk down the road from the church, go round the first RH hair-pin bend and then just after the next LH bend take the wide gravel track leading off to the right heading southwest and marked with faint blue paint marks if you look hard enough. The route is pretty straight forward just keep following the gravel vehicle track along the side of the hill, descending slowly.

2) Pass through several wire gates. Pass an old, abandoned WV camper van (if it's still there) despite wishful inspection it looks beyond repair. Pass through the wire gate to its right and continue following the blue dot marks. After a short distance, the track starts to ascend.

3) The track starts a series of turns and climbs up through some olive groves. At the top of the first LH bend is an old abandoned collapsed church with a bell still eerily hanging in the bell frame. Pass the church keeping right through another wire gate with the legend "please close the door". The track now becomes more like a wide path, turning right, climbing and then left.

4) Follow the path around the end of the hill, ignore a path off to the left. The path becomes quite narrow with lots of scrub. Stay with the blue dots which are joined by yellow dots as the path turns to head northeast over the rise. Clear views can be seen to the south and Paleochora comes into view.

To your right is the fort where we are headed. There is a wire fence to your right and the path stays to the LH side of it.

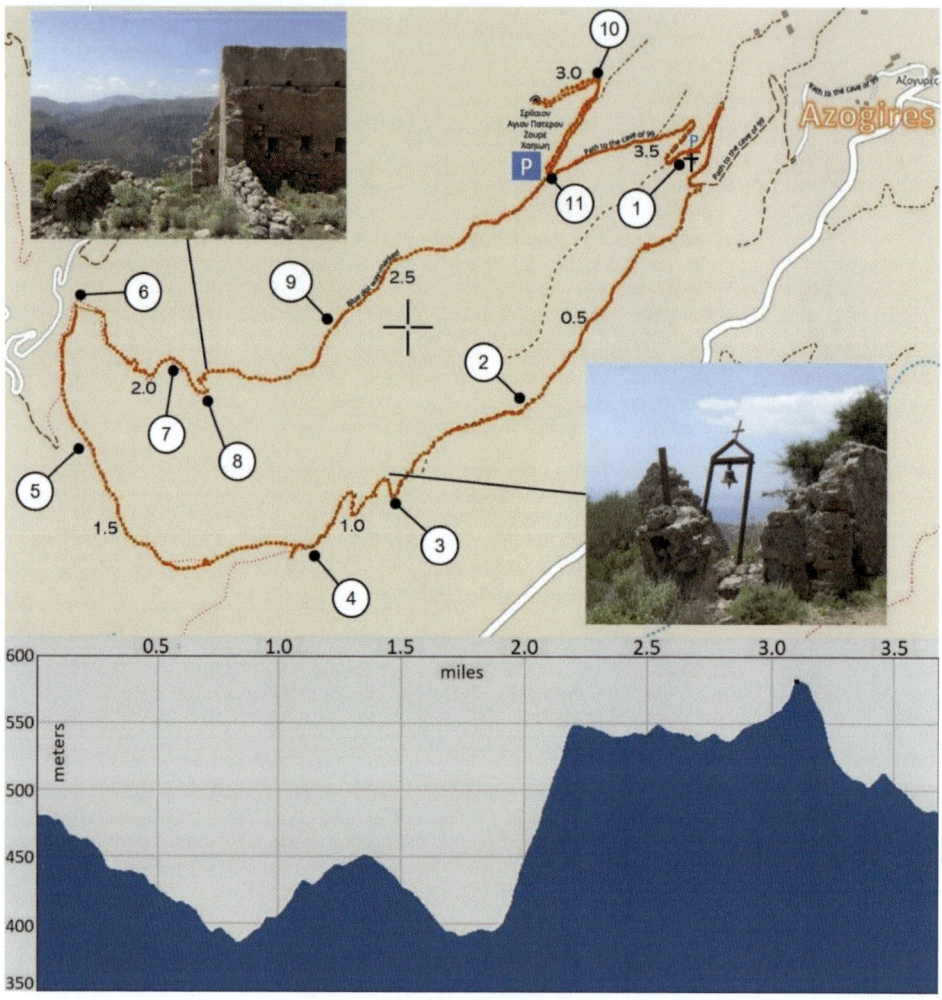

5)   The path stops descending as you turn around the hillside heading more northwards. There is an interesting walled cave just above the path that seems to be used for keeping goats by the smell of it! Heading down to where the path levels off you reach the back of some buildings and follow a wall to its end.

6)   At the end of the wall turn right to find a path climbing upwards. There are red paint way markers, but these are difficult to see. Where the path starts to become indistinct you need to go up and over to the right using goat paths, through bushes and trees, which is difficult and steep. Keep going upwards the best way you can, it is actually not that far through the bushes and trees and come out on a steep sloping section that needs to be negotiated to reach the Fort. We found our own way up the hillside which may not have been the best way to go and you might choose better routes. My route will take you to a wire gate in the top RH corner of a fenced enclosure that needs to be found to get access to the open hillside.

View up to the fort, approach to the right

Looking down into the cave entrance

Shrine on the floor of the cave

7) Work your way up to the Fort around the rock formations as best you can, heading towards the RH side of the Fort where there is a gate in the fence.

8) The Fort can only be accessed from the eastern side, so you need to go around the RH side to the back. The views here are excellent and it's an obvious place for a rest and to take in the ambience. To leave the Fort retrace your steps to the western side through the gate, go along the side of the Fort to a gate and find a blue dot marked path that leads to the Cave of 99 Saints.

9) Keep following the blue dot marked path. It is clear to see and arrives at the Cave/Fort parking area where the cave is signposted.

10) Find the path to cave at the north side of the parking area. Climb up the path to the cave through the saddle and then down again to the entrance. There are a series of rusty ladders leading down into the cave and care must be taken on the ladders and the slippery surfaces. Use your judgement as to whether it safe for you. There are sometimes lights. At the bottom is the shrine to the 99 Holy Fathers along with the guano and smells of many pigeons; maybe it should be the Cave of 99 Pigeons. Further on the cave is almost completely filled with a large fallen boulder. There is a very tight passage down the side of the boulder which leads to a much larger open area, so I'm told. I got as far as trying to squeeze past the boulder but become too 'cautious' to continue.

11) To return to the start point, re-trace the route to the Cave/Fort parking area and turn left down the road.

H. Krios, Three Beaches

Distance	4.5 miles, 7.2 km.
Ascent	322m, 1090 ft
How to Get There	Krios beach is just under 6 miles west of Paleochora. There is a labyrinth of poorly signposted roads for the last 3 miles used to service the greenhouses. It is best to use Google maps or some such, or a paper map for directions. However, you can try and follow these directions: Take the west coast road out of Paleochora signposted Kountoura 6km leaving the town. After passing many beaches you come to a part where the road climbs up a tight turn left and then a sharp right. Afterwards, follow the road around to the left and pass a restaurant on your right opposite a glass-fronted shop on the left. Keep going, now in open country and after a straight climb, white buildings appear on a sharp RH turn. There is a signpost pointing right for 'Voutas 18' and 'Sklavopoula 11'. Ignore the sign and go straight on off the bend. Stay on this 'straight' road and at the end follow it around to the right and then the left. At the next T junction turn left and follow the road around the 90 deg RH bend at the end. At the next junction turn left for the service road down to Krios beach.
Start Point	Car Parking area at Krios beach

Description

This is provided as a circular walk, but you can use it just to visit one or more of the beaches and return via the same route. The word beach is used loosely here. Krios beach is pebbly but quite large and accommodating. There is a bar there, car parking areas and showers. The beach is divided in two by a large rock formation which can be easily climbed to access the western part used by nudists. Viena beach is a small shallow and rocky harbour, there is some sand at the western end but only room for a couple of families. The significant attraction of Viena beach is the ancient stone columns lying on the shore. Looking around it is easy to find shards of pottery. The church/temple that was once there is predicted to be 3rd Century AD. There is now a notice board providing information. It is a very tranquil and peaceful place. The Red Sand Beach is at the bottom of a cove. It is another pebble beach, arrived at by steep goat paths. The attraction of this beach is that it is very secluded, and you normally have the place to yourselves. The ascent probably puts most people off, either that or they are more set on walking to/from Elefonisi to detour down into the cove.

Walk Directions

1) Climb over the large rock formation dividing the beach to access the west side of the beach. Walk to the end of the beach and take the path climbing up, over and around large rocks. Always look for the well-trodden route avoiding difficult obstacles. After a short distance, arrive out on to the open hillside with the path heading up the hillside going northeast. Remain on this path to arrive at and join a wide gravel track heading east-west, turn left along the track (incidentally, by turning right you can use this track as an easier return option up to a church and back down to the car park, avoiding the beach). The track takes you up through the saddle of two hills. As the track levels off meet a righthand turn to a steep, straight gravel track heading north. This route can be taken as a short cut to the Red Sand Beach avoiding walking down to Viena beach at sea level and climbing back up again. To continue to Viena beach follow the route straight ahead down to the beach. This is the E4 route and the yellow and black markings can be found here and there.

2) As the track descends, leave it taking a path descending further down to the left, heading straight to Viena beach. The path starts to level off approaching bushy scrub land area. There are many paths here, but the Viena bay destination can be seen in the distance for guidance. The route remains parallel with the shore before turning down towards the bay partially along a gulley. Explore the bay, maybe take a dip, then continue your journey by picking up the E4 again at the far end of the

Ancient columns on the shore at Vienna Beach

bay, walking past the sandy little bay to the left on the other side of the bay. Climb up from Viena beach on a more or less straight path heading for a ridge to the left of a prominent rock outcrop.

3) After reaching the top of the ridge the route curves around to the right. There's a little climbing up and down and one part where there is a steep loose slope to cross. It is not far to cross it and not as bad as it may seem. Round the headland to get great views along the coast to Elefonisi. Keep following the E4 route along the hillside until you arrive at the church of St John.

4) The church is a good place to take a rest, there are picnic tables and a water tap. The church is in a fenced compound which is within another fenced area. To get to the beach pass the outer compound on the LH side and when at the bottom of the fenced area make your way to the right effectively moving behind the church again. There are many goats (and human) routes here but take those which look most used down towards the beach. The route becomes better defined as the beach approaches. Just keep heading downwards and towards the right and you can't go far wrong. After visiting the beach make your way back to the church. This time when at the church take the route heading straight up the hill to the left of the

Route down to the Red Beach and view to Elafonisi

approach route. Keep ascending on this clear wide track heading to a rocky lookout point at the peak. Taking this route back halves the amount of climbing compared to retracing the route through Viena beach.

5) At the peak enjoy the great views out to sea. From here, walk along a ridge with views to both sides. After the ridge, continue on the track and descend. There are a couple of junctions on the way down, on both occasions keep right. The track will bring you down to the original route from the start, use this to retrace your steps back to Krios beach. There is the option to remain on the same track back to the car park, as mentioned earlier past the church, rather than take the steep rocky route down to the western end of the beach that you came up on. The choice is yours.

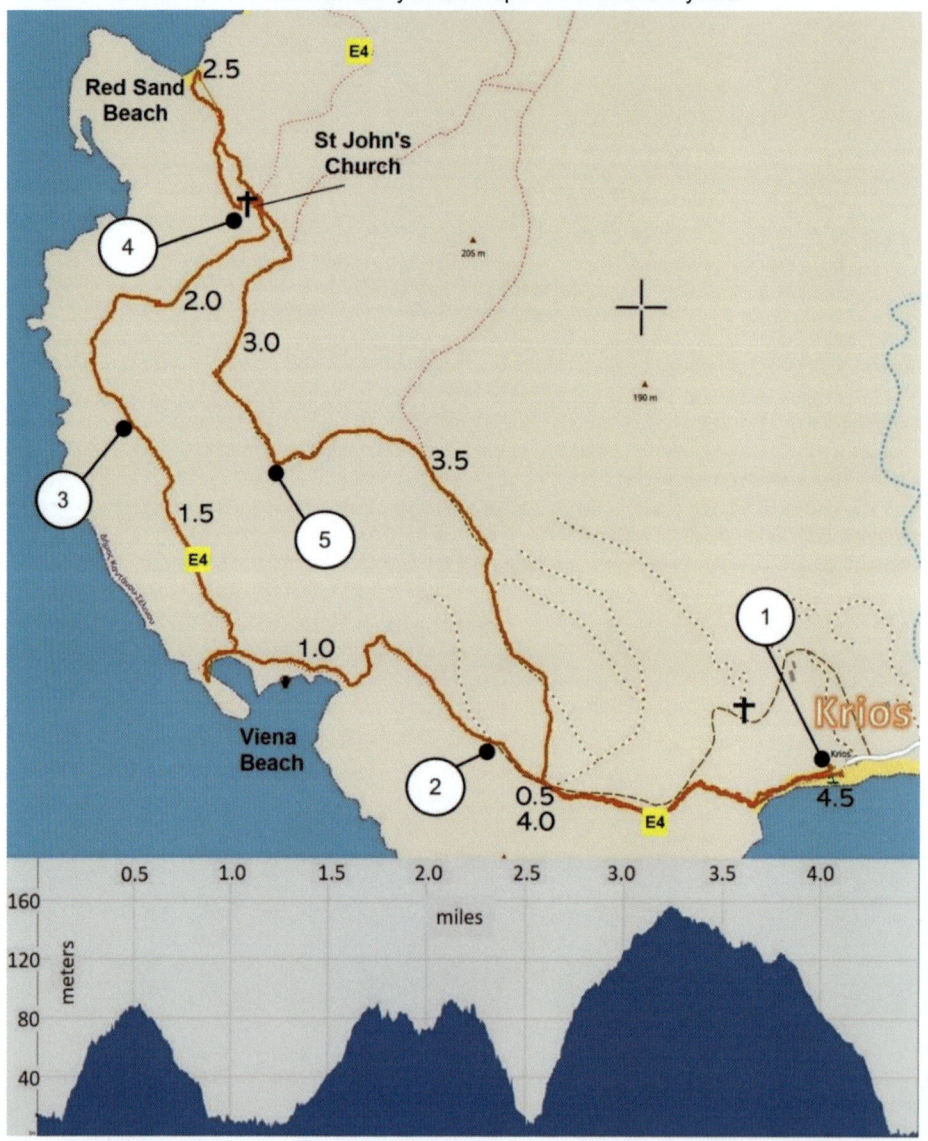

I. Voutas to Karavopetra beach via the Ridge Tombs

Distance	6.2 miles, 10 km
Ascent	194m, 636 ft (Descent 472m, 1550ft)
How to Get There	Take the Voutas and Sarakina road turning right from the western Paleochora beach road as it leaves town. After 7.5km, at a junction with Sarakina signposted straight ahead 4km and Voutas left around a sharp LH bend over a bridge. Take the road to Voutas. A further 3.8km after the junction on approaching Voutas, there is a church on the RH side of the road above a stone wall after a 90 degree LH bend. A little further on there is another church on the LH side of the road if you reach this turn round and go back.
Start Point	Just before the church on the RH side of the road is a wide track heading down the hillside on the LH side of the road. The start point is the entrance to this track.

Description

This is a linear walk that is worth the inconvenience because of the dramatic views down the Pelakaniotikes valley and the atmospheric ancient rock tombs cut into the ridge halfway along. It is mainly descent with marginal ascent. I would like to point out the GPS elevation chart between 2.5 and 3.0 miles has clearly gone a bit off message. It really is not as extreme as shown and probably can be put down to trees blocking the signal. Being linear, you will need to arrange a taxi or bus to the start and probably a taxi home although the road distance back to Paleochora centre is only a further 2.25 miles (3.62km) if you wish to walk back.

Walk Directions

1) Walk down the track from the road, heading initially towards Voutas and then taking a sharp left to follow the contours of the valley and the route of the river below, more-or-less. For the next 2 miles it is a clear route remaining on this track, do not take any side-tracks or paths.

2) At 2 miles you will pass a gravel track joining your track from the left. A little after this, just under 100m, is an important detour where you leave your track and climb a rocky path up the hillside to the left. It is easy to miss this path. It starts to the left of a large grey boulder on the left of the track (pictured). There is a faint blue arrow painted on the boulder pointing left and a little way up the path is marked with blue and white paint.

3) The path climbs straight up the hillside initially, heading to the left of a high rock formation. Circle around the back of these rocks turning right and then left to follow the path southwards. Stay to the left of a fence and follow the blue markers along this atmospheric and most likely ancient route. It is about 700m to the first of the rock tombs.

4) The first tombs to find are on the right cut into the rocky ridge a little above the most used path route (there are lots of goat tracks). Another 50m on or so, there is another group of tombs the most spectacular of which is open at the end providing a view straight through to the valley beyond. To continue, simply keep following the path down to a church.

5) Pass the LH side of the church to arrive at an open area with a tall bell tower. Attempt to resist the urge to ring the bell. The church interior is much older than the external appearance would suggest. There is a gravel track here, down to the road which could be used to just visit the tombs; without doing the whole walk, parking at the bottom and walking up. Continue heading south on the main track which continues for three miles or so to the main coast road.

6) You will come to a part where the way ahead is blocked by a fence with a Keep Out notice. Here turn right, climb a little to then zig-zag down the wide gravel track on the other side of the hill and turn left at a junction. Now circle to your left still descending to come to a location almost opposite where the route would have arrived if allowed to have gone straight ahead at the Keep Out notice.

7) At another junction turn sharp right to start heading south again and ascend another rise. The track starts to descend again and will bring you eventually down to the main coast road to Paleochora. From here it is a taxi or walk back to Paleochora.

Tombs cut directly into rock on the ridge

J. Voutas Churches

Distance	6.4 miles, 10.3km
Ascent	452 m, 1780ft
How to Get There	Take the road signposted to Voutas from the western coast road leaving Paleochora. Going through Voutas turn left where there is a blue road sign pointing right to Chania 68km and Strovles 15km. Turn left signposted Sklavopoula 8, Elefonisi 17 but you don't see it until you've committed to the turning. Follow the road turning right through houses out of the village. After a few bends, the road becomes relatively straight. Pass the LH turning to Chasi 2km. Stay on the straight road and pass a large white house on the left, after that arrive at a sharp LH bend. Park at the Layby on the RH side of the bend with the Church of St. Friday opposite on the inside of the bend.
Start Point	At the Church of St Friday

Description

A peaceful walk that starts at the amazing 14th century church of St. Friday and meanders around the valley and through shady olive groves and to other small settlements with views across the valley and churches along the way. The Church of St Friday has some very alarming and graphic murals which are not to be missed.

Walk Directions

Church of St Friday

1)   Climb the steps to the church and enter it to see the amazing 14th century wall frescoes depicting scenes from hell, quite extraordinary. After having a good look around leave the church via the entrance steps to the road below. At the road, turn left and follow the road until reaching the

first turning left. Along the way to the right in the valley can be seen an old concrete viaduct.

2)   The LH turn is signposted Kittypo (yes really), take this road and climb the hill.

3)   Keep following the road uphill at the start of a 180-degree RH bend there is a track off to the right that leads to another church. I must admit that it wasn't until looking at the map afterwards that I realised that we missed this church, but it may well be worth a look, returning to the road afterwards. Keep following the road, to go round a 180degree bend to the left after the RH one. After a while come to a junction with the road bending sharply to the

right, do not turn but keep straight on between a high stony wall on your right and a lower one on the left. This is the road to Kittypo.

Inside all Saints Church

4)   At Kittypo, opposite the first white concrete building on the left, there is a path climbing up through the olive groves on your right. Heading right at an acute angle to the road initially climbing up past the red corrugated roof of a building below. Follow the path up alongside dry-stone walls and it will bring you to another church just before joining a gravel road. The church is worth having a peek inside, it is called All Saints and indeed there is a picture inside with many saints. From the church turn left along the gravel road and keep on it for just over 1km before turning off.

5)   After about 800m there is a sharp hairpin bend to the right followed by a 180-degree LH bend and then the track remains relatively straight. Leave the car track on another track to the right which initially rises over the bank before then dropping down into a valley. Where this turning is there is a fence on your left and a slight change in direction of the road to the left. If you find yourself following the track left and then right, you have passed and missed the track on the right.

6)   The track now follows the side of the valley descending slowly at first and steeper later. The route goes to the head of the valley and back along the other side to the village of Langadas which can be seen directly opposite and to the right. The track is reasonably clear and straightforward as it meanders around the valley. There are some minor routes off but in all cases stay with the main track.

7)   As Langadas approaches the track becomes concrete before ending at a junction with a tarmac road, turn left at the junction. There is another church in Lagadas should you wish to visit. Stay on this road climbing for 1.4km before turning off.

8)   The road takes you along the side of another valley to the village of Kalamiou. The road to Paelochora can be seen on the other side of the valley. After passing the sign for Kalamiou and shortly afterwards a white concrete house on the right, take the turn right on the apex of a LH hairpin bend, down a concrete road to the heart of the village.

9)   Enter the village and arrive at a little gathering area with white walls and tap under a shady tree, a good place to take a break. From here follow the road which turns right out of the gathering area passing the houses. Ignore the RH turn which appears almost immediately carrying straight past a building on the right and a high stone wall on your left. Carry on further and take the next concrete road on the right, straight ahead goes to the church. On turning right there is an interesting traditional stone farm building on the left with rusty metal grids in the windows. The concrete immediately ends, and it becomes a gravel road. Ignore a RH turn and keep left with a stone wall on the left going around a RH bend. Stay on this track.

Turn right and pass this old building

10) After 350m take a RH fork down the hillside. This is a shortcut through to the track ahead which zig-zags down the valley, but we do not re-join the track, turning off right just before we get there on another path initially heading down and then levelling off.

11) The path starts to climb again and then steeply up onto the main track above which is concrete where we join it. Turn left along the track. Follow the route around the hillside ignoring paths off to the left along the way. The route becomes an open area before re-entering trees to come across the Church of Saint Spyridon after passing a large olive tree with a broken wall at its base. Go past the church (with it on your right) to a gate to the church courtyard, enter the courtyard and find another good place for a rest and an opportunity to explore the church. We leave via the main access track for the church with the church entrance behind us.

12) The church track ends where it joins a road, turn left to follow the road back to the start point.

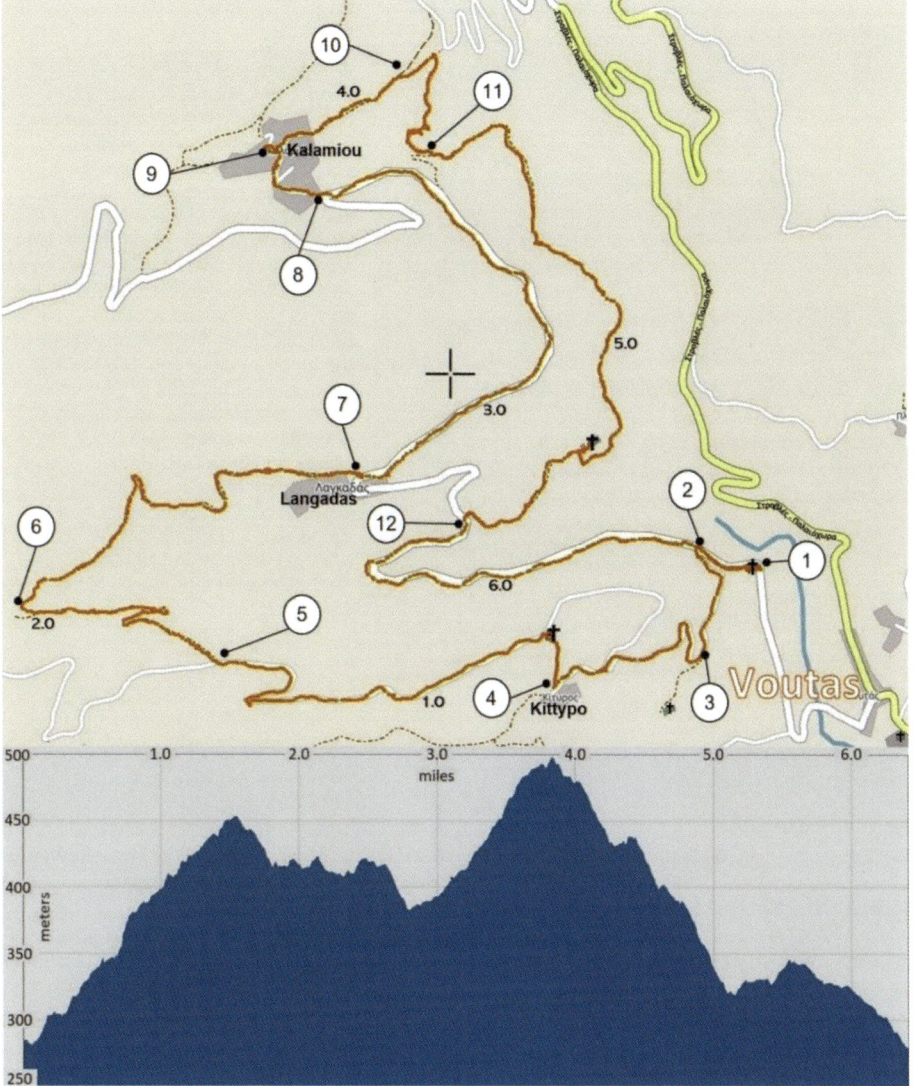

K. Kandanos Churches and Ancient Tree

Distance	4.9 miles, 7.9km (yellow route). Option for additional loop (green route) for 6.6 miles, 10.6km.
Ascent	Yellow route 282m, 925ft. Total with green route 327m, 1071ft
How to Get There	Take main Chania road from Paleochora to Kandanos
Start Point	The main Plaza of Kandanos
Car Parking	When entering the town there are parking spaces on the RH side of the road, next to an open plaza

Description

'The church of Ascension'

A pleasant walk whether you take the shorter or longer option starting in Kandanos which is an attractive town with a dark history. The walk takes you through the town, into olive groves and past churches where you can visit or stop in the shade. The ultimate destination being the ancient Monumental Olive Tree of Kandanos said to be thousands of years old. Be sure to stop for a drink at the beginning or end of the walk in one of the friendly restaurants and find the memorial on the edge of the main Plaza. The plaques there explain about the complete destruction of the village and the killing of about 180 of its inhabitants on 3 June 1941 by German occupying forces during World War II. There is also a museum which explains more, located in the city hall next to the Church of the Ascension.

Route Options

There is one main route shown with an orange trace on the map and the option of an additional 2 mile loop shown with a green trace on the map.

Walk Directions

1) Leave the town on the main road heading towards Paleochora with the plaza on the left. Where the road bears around to the left take the RH road running tangential off the corner descending, signposted The Church of Ayios Ioannis. Remain on this narrow descending road.

2) The road is a relatively straight descent with RH and LH turn at the end. After which, there is a fork in the road with a sign pointing left to the church. Our route takes us right up the side road. However, the church is not far and it is worth making a visit and return should you choose.

3) Follow the road up from the junction. After a tight RH bend and before another RH 90 degree bend take the LH turning (green route) ascending past some buildings on the RH side, stay on this track ignoring routes off to the left. If doing the shorter orange route, keep straight ahead around the 90 degree bend and jump to step 7. Pass the buildings turning right and the road deteriorates to a

gravel track. Keep on this track ignoring any turnings off until you exit onto the main Paleochora-Chania Road.

4) On reaching the road turn right heading back towards Kandanos. Follow the road around a long LH bend and then a right before it straightens with grapes growing in the fields either side of the road before our turning off on the right.

5) Halfway around the next LH bend take the tarmac road on the right, (just after an earth layby on the right where farm produce is sold) doubling back on yourself. It might still be signposted 'Vineyards of Kandanos'. Grapes can be seen again growing either side of the road, how they are cultivated is quite different from what is usually seen in mainland Europe. After about 400m the road turns left around the first of two sharp LH bends, the second after a further 300m. The first is about 90 degrees the second is almost 180 degrees.

6) Just after the second LH bend ignore the turning right. Stay on the tarmac road and on reaching a 'T' junction turn left. You have now joined up with the shorter orange route option.

7) Follow the road through the houses to reach another junction and turn right. The road now takes a slow LH turn to an excellent traditional old stone building on your left just before turning a RH bend. Stay on this road.

8) After a sharp RH bend, come to a junction with a left turn and a sign pointing to the church of Ayios Mamas straight ahead. It is worth visiting the church which has a large shelter from the sun with concrete seating, a good place for a rest. After visiting the church return to the junction and turn right. Follow the road up to the main road out of Kandanos and turn left towards Chania.

9) Pass a community olive pressing factory on the right followed by a school. Just after the school at the end of a stone wall take the concrete road turning right (marked as a path on the map) signposted to the Church of Michaechagelos.

10) When you come to a sharp RH turn in the road with a gravel track straight ahead, ignore the gravel track, turning right and continuing to follow the road.

11) Follow the road up the hill round a slight LH bend. At the start of a sharp 180 degree RH, hairpin bend, take a LH turn just before the bend to the Church of Michaechagelos.

12) Enjoy your visit to the church. The route now exits to the left of the front of the church through a small metal gate in the church yard wall. Follow this low, dry walled path taking a RH turn after a short distance up to the road above and turn left along the road.

13) Follow this road for about 700m through a series of bends when it straightens. 2/3rds along the straight take the LH turn for the road to the monumental Olive tree. There is a sign on the RH side of the road with an arrow pointing left announcing "Monumental Olive Tree of Kandanos". Follow the road through some houses and keep straight on ignoring any RH or LH turns.

The "Monumental Olive Tree of Kandanos"

14) When you reach a distinct LH bend in the road take the gravel track leading off to the right, signposted to the 'Monumental Olive Tree'. Explore the olive tree estimated to be 3000 years old. There are information notices and walled areas making it an ideal picnic spot.

15) To continue, pass the tree to the path below running alongside a stone wall, turn right and follow the path past a church on the right to meet another path at a T junction. At the T junction turn right and follow this path a short distance to a gravel road and turn left.

Follow the road down to another junction and bear left. The track now becomes straight and turns to tarmac about halfway down. The road meets the main Paleochora-Chania road at the bottom, turn left back to Kandanos and the start point.

L. Kandanos Southern Hills

Distance	6.7 miles, 10.8 km
Ascent	441 m, 1447 ft
How to Get There	Take main Chania road from Paleochora to Kandanos
Start Point	The main Plaza of Kandanos
Car Parking	When entering the town there are parking spaces on the RH side of the road next to an open plaza

Description

An exhilarating walk which starts in the town and then zig-zags up the hill where you will be rewarded with terrific views across the Kandanos valley. Mostly on tracks through woods, uncultivated land and olive groves with a bit of road walking. Very quiet with just a few goats for company.

Walk Directions

1) From the plaza in Kandanos walk along towards the large church behind the LH bend of the main road. There are two restaurant's tables and chairs situated on either side of a side road that approaches the bend apex from the right. Across the side turning are the memorials to the village people who were killed when the village was destroyed by the Germans during WWII. This is worth seeing because they are replicas of the inscriptions placed in the village by the Germans, one of which states "Here stood Kandanos, destroyed in retribution for the murder of 25 German soldiers, never to be rebuilt again". To continue follow the road around the LH bend and walk down Kandanos main street passing the restaurants and shops, looking for the first RH road turning which is a little way along down the side of an ELTA post office.

2) Take the RH turning and proceed up this road for about half a mile where the road splits in two on a LH bend. Take the LH fork signposted 'The Church of Agia Kiriaki' and continue on the road climbing through the trees. Stay on this road for just over another half a mile.

3) After a 90 degree RH bend the road straightens out and you will see a large white concrete house at the end of the road. Walk towards the house and the road turns right in front of it. Do not turn right but head up the path to the left of the house between some black ornate railings on the right and a nice stone wall on the left, (on the map it shows that we did turn right in order to look at the large traditional stone building on that road before returning to the route).

4) Just past the side of the house turn left and follow a narrow climbing path through the undergrowth beneath trees. The route climbs alongside a cleft in the ground to the RH side. Admittedly this path can become overgrown but is still traceable. If in doubt move to the higher ground on the left before then heading to the right and climbing steeply to bring you out onto a wide loose stone track.

5) On reaching the track turn left and follow it around the hillside. There are now good views back across the Kandanos valley. On a sharp hairpin bend follow it left ignoring the lesser path off the bend straight ahead. After about 550m and after a LH bend take a sharp RH turn, again ignoring the track straight ahead which has a wire gate across it with a sign on it. We think it says 'close the gate' but the letters are very warn.

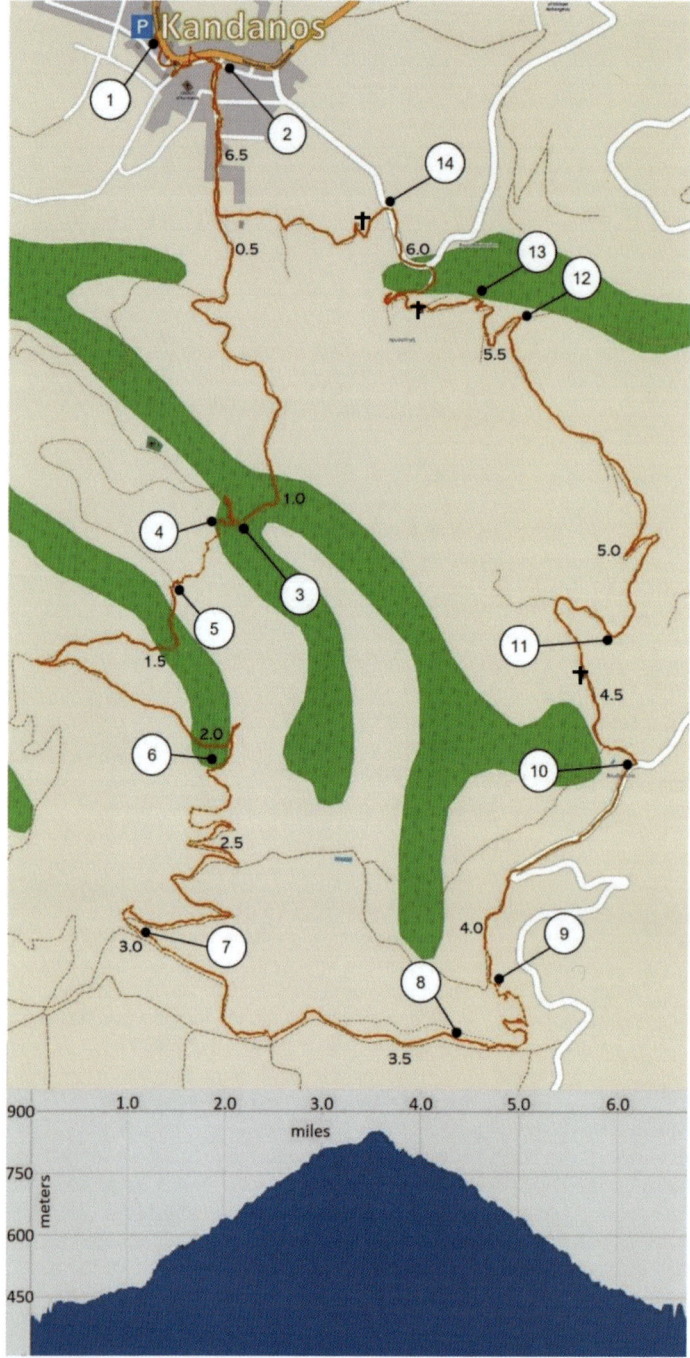

6) Approach a large steel gate that completely blocks the track, there is a chain holding it closed but the padlock is not used. Pass through the gate and make sure it is secured how you found it. Entering an orderly olive grove. Turn left turn and follow the track around the side of the main grove curving around to the right. The track straightens and goes into the centre of the grove, take the wide track left through the tress to the wide track on the other side and turn left again. Take this new track to the end where it turns sharp right to immediately reach a track going across in front of you, turn right and follow it around another LH hairpin bend up to a gate marking the exist of the grove. Beyond the gate is the main track, turn right and follow this track in large zig-zags up the hillside.

7) The track ends when it reaches a T junction with another track. Turn left along the new track and the ascent will now decrease significantly. At the next junction turn left along the top of the hill. After a RH bend, there is a 70m stretch of concrete to assist vehicles up the steep incline to reach the summit and the highest part of the walk.

8) Descending past a solar power farm on the right, looking down the track from here to see it descends and then starts climbing again. Where it reaches the bottom is our turning to leave the track on the left. After turning off left follow the new

Ladder in fence behind tree

track turning to the left, ignore the track going straight ahead off the curve up the hill. Keep on this track and it will turn sharp right into a wooded area. There is a small ravine on the left, go to the head of the ravine and turn left to cross it and follow the path on the other side. When amongst the trees head downwards keeping to the right of the ravine, do not descend to the bottom of it. Also, do not climb up right to the road above. Keep heading down to where the ravine is crossed by a wide track at the bottom. There is a strong fence preventing access to the track but hidden behind a large tree there is a small metal ladder built into the fence to allow escape.

9) After climbing over the fence walk down to the track and turn right. Continue along the side of the hill with great views west across the valley, keep going to reach a road on a hairpin bend. Turn left at the road and follow it downhill. Walk down to the small village of Vamvakades on the LH side of the road. Take the LH turn on a RH bend with a concreted turning off to a track that goes behind a large concrete house. It is the only house on the bend.

View over Kandanos from the solar farm

10) Pass the village houses and go through the fence-gate at the end of a tall stone wall on the left. Keep going to come to a well-kept small church with an exposed bell tower. Pass the church on the RH side, remain on this track and follow it through the trees, after the trees follow the bend around to the right ignoring the turning off to the left at a junction. Remain on this track descending into trees again to a junction where the ground levels off.

11) At the junction turn left for the track that takes you almost all the way back to Kandanos. After a large zig-zag, the route comes out on to the open hillside again.

12) As you round the end of the hill take the LH turning heading downwards, heading back on yourself, southwest. After a LH bend the track narrows to a grassy path, ignore the path approaching up from the left.

13) The tack comes down to a 'T' junction (not shown on the map) with a track running across in front with a fence on the other side. Turn left and descend to a rather grand church right in the middle of the track. Navigate around the church to the right and join the concrete church access road. Take this concrete road down to the tarmac road below and turn right. This road leads to the main road passing an interesting slightly abandoned white concrete building with a sign that translates to 'Printing House'. At the main road turn left.

14) Head down the road to the road sign indicating the end of the village of Koufalotos. Take the track on the left just before this sign where there is a much smaller wooden sign pointing to 'Noly Apostles'. Follow the path around a RH bend to the church and then take the left turning away from the church, and then a turn right. This path now leads all the way back to the road that this walk used to leave Kandanos at the start. At a path junction about 200m from the church, turn right. On reaching the road turn right and return to Kandanos. It is suggested that you now avail yourselves to a well-deserved cold beer, and/or the delights at the ice cream parlour.

7. Drive
M. Milia

Distance	6.0 miles, 9.7 km
Ascent	461 m, 1512 ft
How to Get There	Take the main Chania road from Paleochora that passes through Kantanos. After ~10.6km in Pelmeniana take the left turn (2km before Kandanos) signposted Elefonisi 38km. Stay on this road. After 8.1km at a junction turn right, signposted Elafonisi 31km. After a further 3.3 Km at a T junction, you meet the main Kissamos-Elefonisi road. Here turn right towards Kissamos (Elefonisi is left). Pass the Silk fuel station and take the next LH turn signposted to Rogdiga and Vlatos. Stay on this road for 2.3km. Look out for a brown wooden signpost on the RH side with white lettering saying MHΛIA 4550km pointing right. This is just before a large unfinished white concrete house on the LH side. Take the next turning right opposite another MHΛIA sign on the LH side. Now stay on this road and at each junction look for the sometimes small brown and white wooden signs for directions and it will take you to Milia.
Start Point	The visitors' car park at Milia village.

Description
Milia is a village that can trace its origins back to the 15th Century. It was rebuilt in 1990 using traditional methods and crafts. It is a mountain retreat with an excellent restaurant that has a terrace with views overlooking the mountainous valleys. More information can be found at https://www.milia.gr/milia-history/. The village is located high in the mountains so you know there will be spectacular views, at times glimpsing Kissamos bay. Be sure to spend some time exploring the village and taking some refreshments on the terrace after your walk. NB: On this walk, you will need to twice climb over a strong wire fence just over a metre high.

Walk Directions
1) Leave the car park via the road you entered. Stay on the road around the bend and climb the hill out of the village. Stay on this road for about 1km before turning off. After the second RH bend with great views out across the valley, the road straightens out. Still climbing a ridge ahead extending to the left comes into view with a large white concrete structure on it and a smaller lookout building beyond it. This is where the route turns left off the road.

2) At the junction with the ridge turn left through the fence-gate to follow a route to the left of the fence just below the ridge. To be clear, the route is not taking the higher parallel track to the right of the fence that leads to the two buildings. That being said, it is worth visiting the second fire watch building for the views and then return to the route. After passing through the fence-gate follow the ridge route, it is very wide in places and will eventually descend steeply down to a road below.

3) The descent to the road below can be a little tricky with a steep slope and loose stones. We found that it was best to go to the LH side to access the road just before a large gate to another track off the road to the left. Our route takes us through this gate on a track marked with black and yellow markers. Head through the gate, descending to first arrive at a hairpin bend, there are good views down the valley. Follow the track around the bend and continue descending it is a wide track that goes to the eastern side of Milia.

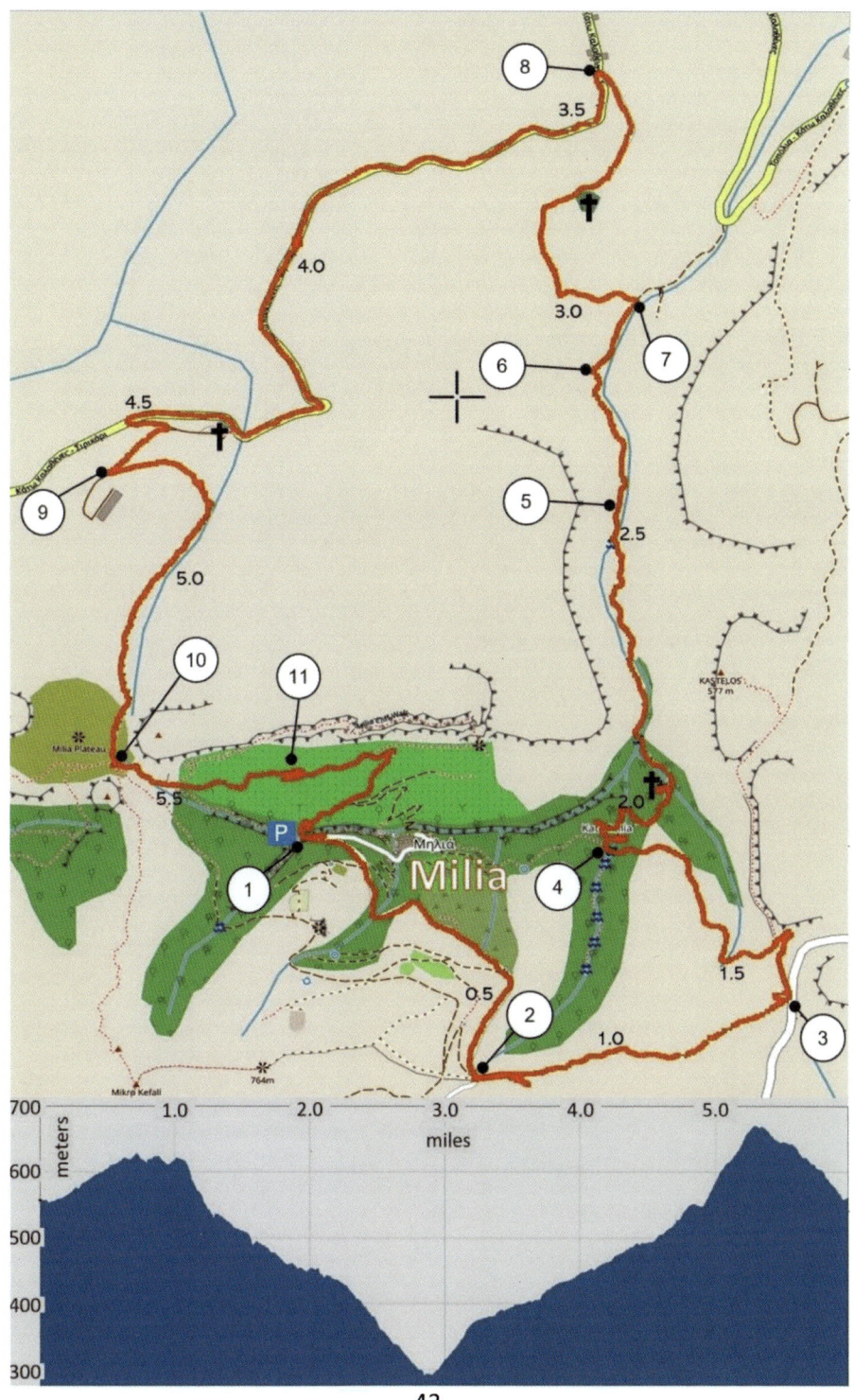

4) Follow the track down towards the village and cross a stream that is sometimes dried up through trees. After the stream, follow the track right (north) and after a short distance, a large collection of beehives can be seen ahead and to the left. Give the beehives a wide berth passing them to the right. Passing through some trees keep going to a church on the left, which is worth a visit. Keep heading north past the church on the main track out of the village. The next turning is 0.8 of a mile or 1290m from the church so you may wish to start measuring the distance because there are no clear markers.

5) After just under half a mile and crossing the river, there is a pair of high metal gates right across the track, they look locked but can be opened, please remember to close them after you.

6) The track arrives at an olive grove where, ignoring the lesser route straight head turn right to continue on the main northbound track. The main descent is now over and the track starts to level off.

7) Just as the track starts to ascend a little take the sharp turning left at a junction and start climbing again. (If you come to a tarmac road you have gone too far and need to return to find the turning which is just after the first LH turn when retracing your steps.) Stay on this ascending track. At a sharp RH bend, ignore the turning off to the left. Shortly after this, the track surface has been concreted. Pass a large well-kept church with a graveyard on the right, after which our track joins a road.

8) At the road turn left. Stay on this road for 1.12 miles, (1.8km) before reaching the turning off to the left. The road is a continuous climb and after a RH hairpin bend come to another RH bend with a long straight concrete service ramp climbing off to the left with railings up to a large white building which is a monastery (but doesn't look like it). Don't take the service ramp but continue on the road turning right then left. As the road straightens out take the sharp LH turn on a road going to the back of the monastery. After a short distance turn right off the road onto a gravel track climbing southwest.

9) As the track climbs there is a bank on the LH side. Look for a small path climbing back against your direction up the bank. Take the path and it climbs and levels out. Continuing in the path's direction and it leads to a fenced-off area with a shed in it. The route is unclear here but the objective is to get to the shallow cleft in the hills behind the shed, climbing north to south across our direction of travel. We found the best way was to climb over and walk to the left of the fence that runs in front of the shed. Pass the shed and arrive at the cleft which has a strong fence running alongside it. When at the end of the fence to your right, climb over it and walk up (south) with the fence running up the cleft on the LH side. This route climbs to the Milia plateau passing through the saddle between two hills on the way.

Take small path climbing back against your direct

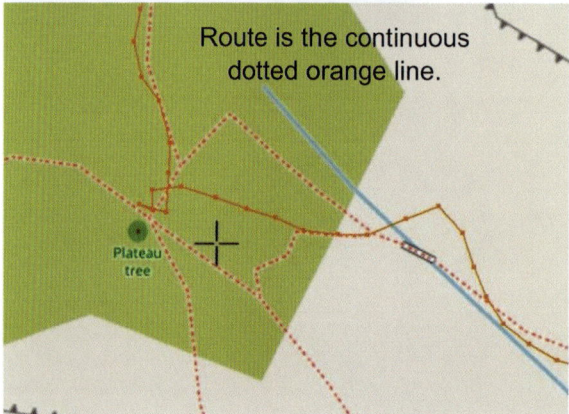

Route is the continuous dotted orange line.

10) After the saddle, descend a little down to a prominent tree on what was once a rough stone wall where many paths converge. Facing the tree looking south there are two paths to the left and one to the right. Neither of these, paths are to be taken. Our route starts heading east a little before we reached the tree. To get to it from the tree take a few steps north (back the way you came) and turn right. It is complicated and there's more than one way of getting to the path, so I've added the map

here to help. The route is marked with red paint dots here and there. The route is now all downhill descending back to Milia.

11) Following the route along and descending the side of the valley arrive at a sharp zig-zag down to a lower level, turning first right and then left. A little further on there is another sharp RH turn where there is also a route ahead that goes to a viewpoint only. Turn right here and the path is more or less straight back down to the Car Park, ignoring paths off to the left. If you haven't already, it's worth exploring the village and the excellent restaurant/cafe.

Entrance to Milia mountain retreat restaurant

N. Milia from Koutsomatados

Distance	7.3 miles, 11.7km
Ascent	655m, 2150ft
How to Get There	Take the main Chania road from Paleochora that passes through Kandanos. After ~10.6km in Pelmeniana take the left turn (2km before Kandanos) signposted Elefonisi 38km. Stay on this road. After 8.1km at a junction turn right, signposted Elafonisi 31km. After a further 3.3 Km at a T junction, you meet the main Kissamos-Elefonisi road. Here turn right towards Kissamos (Elefonisi is left). Your destination is a track on the LH side 3.4km up this road in Koutsomatados, opposite the Kapetanos restaurant before the bends at the Agia Sophia cave.
Start Point	A track on the RH side of the road, just past and up behind a large white house opposite and a little past the Kapetanios restaurant on the other side of the road heading south towards Elefonisi.

Milia traditional village

Description

This walk does not start in Milia but in the small village of Koutsomatados on the main Kissamos-Elephonisi road which overlooks the spectacular Topolia gorge (Walk P). Starting here avoids the long gravel road up to Milia, which is quite rough on small hire cars not designed for that purpose. It also gives you a choice of restaurants to avail yourselves of at the start and finish, with of course a halfway stop at Milia village with its high quality restaurant and mountain views. Take time to visit the Aghia Sophia Cave at the end of your walk, it is well signposted off the main road, climb up the steps to visit the large cave with its stalagmites, stalactites and a small church.

Walk Directions

1) Start ascending the track which runs up to the side and then around the back of the house before turning left to rise steeply and then turn right. You are now presented with a straight, steep climb up to the next bend.

2) After the bend still climbing and circling to the left there are forks to the left and right and middle as the track straightens out. Take the middle steeper track. Incidentally, the RH track takes you to the Aghia Sophia Cave, which is well worth the visit, although it has become over-commercialised in recent times IMHO. Your task is now to keep climbing this steep rocky track for just about 0.8km to the top to meet a tarmac road.

3) On reaching the road turn right a short way, then turn off to the left through a large vehicle gate. You may like to observe that to the west (left) is the return route over the ridge of the hill down to this point. Take the track downwards and notice it is marked with black and yellow markers. At the next hairpin bend, there are good views down the valley. Take the bend and start looking for a turning off to a path on the right.

4) Look for the green and white markers for a path off to the left. The path that doubles back and follows along the hillside supported by a rock wall. Take the turning and keep following this green and white marked route along the side of the valley.

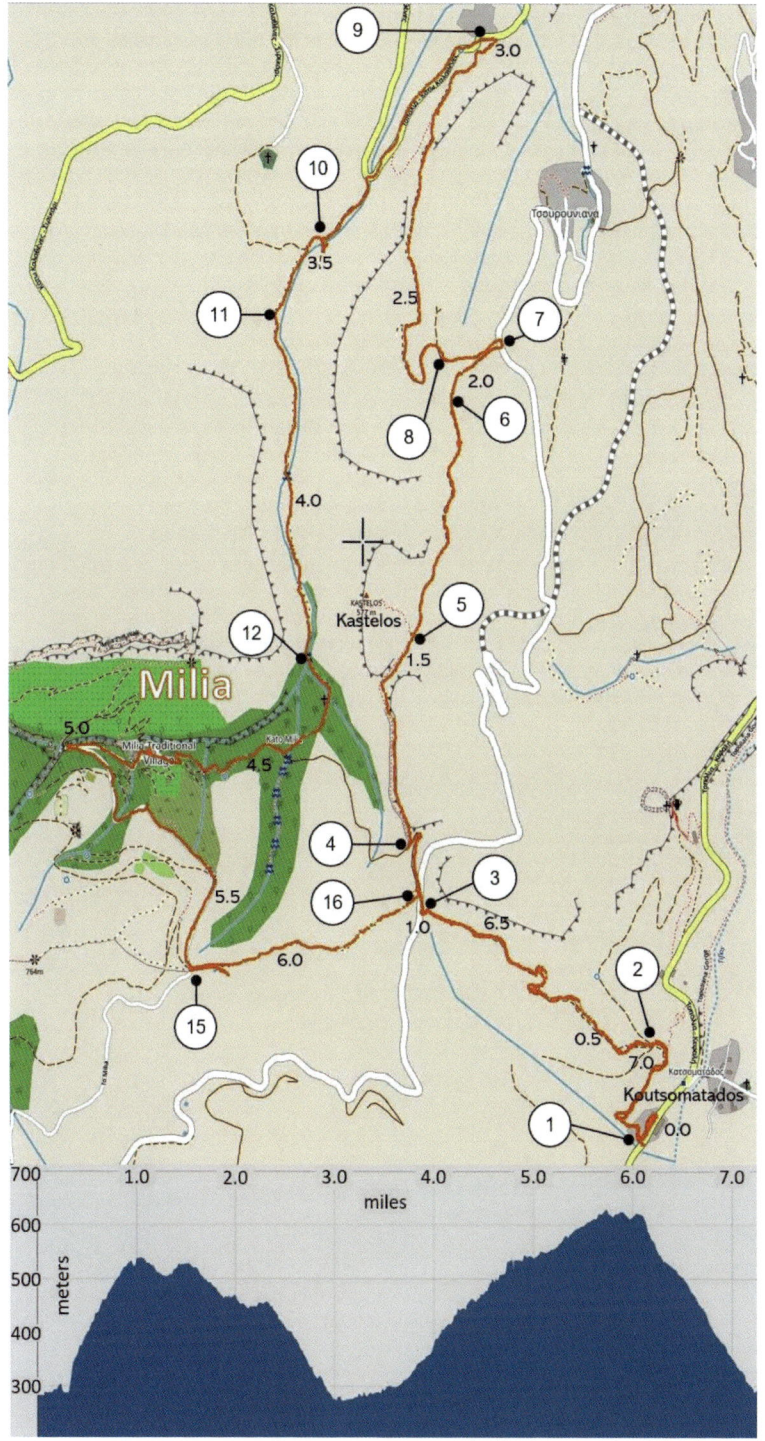

5) The route passes to the right of the peak of Kastelos. There is an opportunity to leave our path and climb up it. If intending to do so, look for a red arrow on a rock to the left of our route adjacent to a peak pointing to the left marking one of the more popular scrambles up to the top. Continuing the walk, stay on the path heading north and ignore any side turnings, heading towards another tarmac road.

6) The road is getting close when the track merges with another track from the right. After which there is a high well-made wire fence on the RH side, mounted on concrete blocks. Keep going as the tracks bends around to the right and down to the road.

7) At the road turn left and left again to come back the way you have just come but on a different track at a lower level.

8) The track bends to the right after which take a LH turning going uphill leaving the main tack which carries on around to the right. Take the rise and level off and at the next junction take the RH rough track curving downwards; rather than carrying on straight ahead. Ignore a LH turning and follow the green and white arrows where they occur. After a RH and then a LH bend the track heads more or less north. Ignore tracks down the hillside to the left and keep going until you meet another road. An aside is that clearly one of these tracks to the left brings you down to the road below, where we are going, but we couldn't determine which one, maybe you can. Either way, the sure route is the one we have taken which is to keep going until you meet the road.

9) At the road you are greeted by some houses. Turn left and walk through the village, carry on until meeting a sharp RH turn where the road crosses the river and heads up the other side of the valley. At the head of the bend leave the road taking the track heading straight on.

10) There is now a combination of bends and forks in the track. Proceed as follows: at a fork in the track on a RH bend, take the RH fork upwards. The track now curves around to the left and another fork in the track appears, here take the LH fork heading downwards.

11) After a few minutes, a low wall appears in front, initially looking as if it is straight across the path. However, a slight turn to the left takes the route past the wall. We are in an olive grove and there are tracks off to the left and right in amongst the trees. Keep to the main path and follow it as it turns right and then left before climbing more or less straight. Carry on and arrive at a formidable tall metal gate across the route, it can be easily unbolted and re-secured to carry on. Keep climbing crossing the river twice to come to a fork. Take the LH route down to cross the river again.

12) Keep straight ahead after the river crossing to enter the outskirts of Milia village, a small church will be seen ahead to the right of the track. Pass the church with it on the RH side and then make your way around to the right passing a safe distance from the beehives on the right, taking a route that keeps the terrace walls above you on the left. At the end of the terrace make your way up to the left to a junction with another route coming from the right. At the junction, turn right following the small path up through the trees. Stay on this path climbing up behind the village winding through the trees to a door framed gate at the top of the climb .

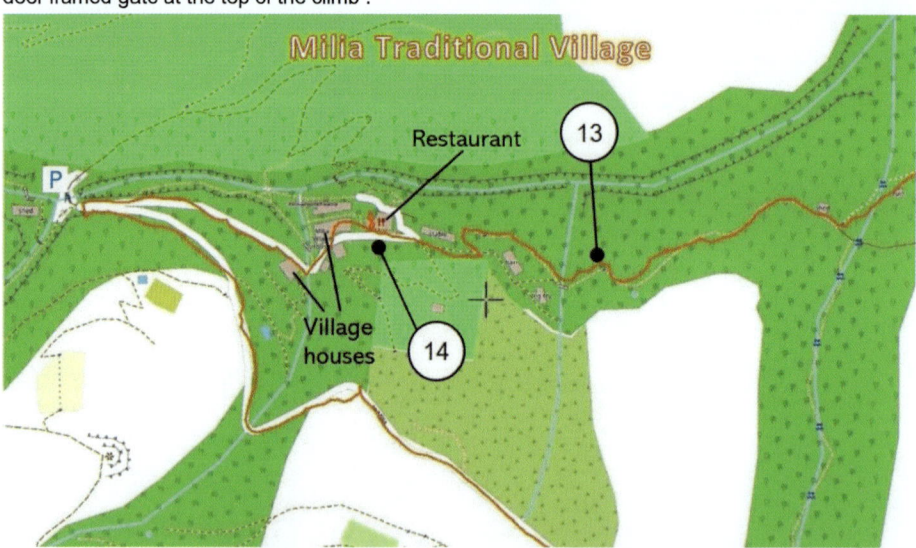

13) Pass through the gate into the pigsty area. Stay on the path, passing with the pigsties on the left. Pass through another door framed gate the other side and then take the steps up left to the main path through the village. Turn right along the main path and walk up to the restaurant. It is highly recommended that you take refreshments there and enjoy the views from the balcony. It is a very atmospheric and relaxing place to be. The dessert menu has some top quality delights.

14) From the restaurant turn right up the hill on the main Milia village road. Follow this gravel road through the houses to a LH hairpin bend at the car park. Stay on the road around the bend and climb the hill out of the village. Stay on this road for about 1km. After the second RH bend, with great views out across the valley, the road straightens out. Still climbing, a ridge ahead extending to the left comes into view with a large white concrete structure on it and a smaller lookout building beyond it.

View of the mountains from the restaurant balcony

15) This is the route back to the start. At the junction with the ridge turn left through the fence-gate to follow a route to the left of the fence just below the ridge. To be clear, you are not taking the higher parallel route to the right of the fence that takes you to the two buildings. That being said it is worth visiting the second lookout building for the views if you choose and then return to the route. After passing through the fence-gate follow the ridge route, it is very wide in places and will eventually leads steeply down to the junction that we were at previously (point 3 on the map), after the main climb up from the start.

Kastelos
Kastelos and Kissamos bay

16) The descent to the junction below can be a bit tricky with a steep slope and loose stones. We found that it was best to go to the left coming out on the road just before the vehicle gate on the left. Once on the main track turn right and then left to descend back to the start point on the track that we originally used to climb out of Koutsomatados. Descend back to the start.

O. Sarakina Valleys

Distance	9.9 miles, 14.4km
Ascent	520m, 1706ft
How to Get There	Take the road signposted to Voutas from the western coast road leaving Paleochora. 8km out of Paleochora there is a sharp LH turn on the other side of a bridge signposted Voutas 4. Do not cross the bridge but turn right signposted Sarakina 4.
Start Point	Sarakina car parking layby as described below.
Car Parking	There's space for parking on the right-hand side of the road just before turning right into the village main road when approaching from the south.

Description

An excellent up and down walk from Sarakina, you start with a steady climb up the side of one valley with great views. The route heads over the top of the ridge to see the valley on the other side with views out to the main Paleochora road. You walk along the side of that valley and then climb back to the ridge and down through the first valley taking in some olive groves along the way. The bar in Sarakina is a friendly local place to stop at the end of your walk.

Walk Directions

1) Heading north to the village from the layby, pass a very well kept church on the right before turning right into the village main street and passing an elevated bar on the left.

2) Just after passing the main village buildings take the narrow concrete track on the right heading down off the main road into the valley.

3) Follow the concrete road around down and around a RH bend at the end of the valley to rise again on the other side and pass some farm processing buildings on the left of the road. After the farm buildings, there are good views back to Sarakina and the hills on the other side of the valley.

4) At the top of the road is a collection of farmhouses, turn left following the track behind a very good example of a typical traditionally constructed stone building.

5) Stay on the main route and ignore minor paths descending to the right, negotiate two 90 degree RH bends, ascending after the second around the hillside.

6) Take the sharp LH turn going up the hillside, ignoring the track going straight ahead to the side of a rusty old square tank with some remaining white paint on it.

7) At another LH bend, ignore the smaller path going straight on; it is a dead end. Keep on zig-zagging your way up the hill.

8) After a while, the track becomes quite straight heading northwards still climbing, you will see the radio mast off to the left ahead which our route passes to the right.

9) As the gravel road starts to level off, you are presented with a fork in the road, stay on the main road keeping left, followed by a LH and then a RH turn.

10) At the top of the climb, the road veers sharp left to go around the side of the adjacent hill to the radio mast. Straight ahead, a rock barrier has been placed to prevent vehicles from using that route. Go straight ahead stepping over the rock barrier and continue on the track descending and following the contours of the hillside. There are great views across the valley from here to the main road through Kallithea.

11) The path becomes increasingly overgrown but is navigable. There are some routes descending to the right, but in all cases keep on the main route around the hillside. After a short distance, the route starts to climb again.

12) On reaching a gravel track turn left followed directly by a RH turn with the vegetation in the road clearing after a wire gate. Go through the gate and keep winding up the hill approaching the

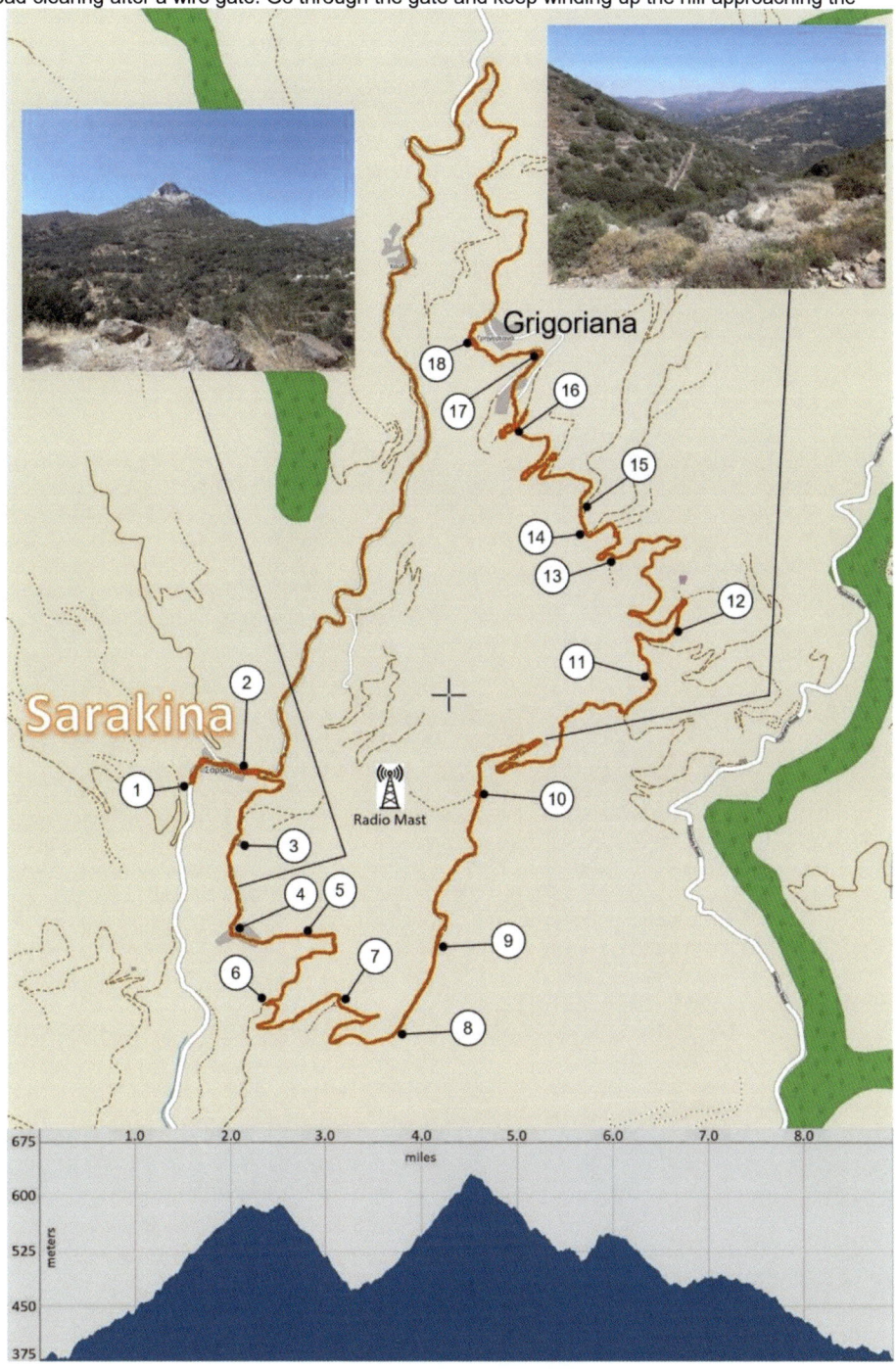

summit.

13) Keep on the main widest track ignore a small path off to the left and head around the sharp RH turn.

14) Ignore routes off to the right and basically keep left or straight on to reach the summit. A great place to take a break and admire the views.

View east from the top

15) When ready, start the descent back into the valley continuing on the same track. There is a fork to the right but keep left heading down the hill.

16) The track zig-zags down the steepest parts of the hill and afterwards becomes concrete. Just after a RH bend, there is a small path doubling back on the left leaving the main route into an overgrown area. Take this path and after a short distance in an opening turn right (N) through some bushes to join a footpath running parallel with the road above. It is a shortcut that avoids the road. Do not worry if you miss it because the two routes join up the other side of Grigoriana. However, it is a shame to miss this pleasant route through the trees.

17) Follow the path past the houses to the head of the valley where it turns left. Keep on the route through the very old olive groves.

18) Where the route starts to descend on a LH bend there is a path climbing steeply to the right. Take the RH path to climb up to a church. At the church, take the concrete steps up to its right. This will bring you out onto the road. The route now is pretty simple. Turn left at the road and follow it down to a stream with a bridge. Cross the bridge and follow the road up to the main road. Turning left at the main road brings you back to Sarakina, where you could stop at the bar for refreshments.

P. Topolia Gorge

Distance	10.7 miles, 17.2 km
Ascent	696m, 2283ft
How to Get There	Take the main Chania road from Paleochora that passes through Kantanos. After approximately 10.6km in Pelmeniana take the left turn (2km before Kantanos) signposted Elefonisi 38km. Stay on this road. After 8.1km at a junction turn right, signposted Elafonisi 31km. After a further 3.3 Km at a T junction, you meet the main Kissamos-Elefonisi road. Here turn right towards Kissamos (Elefonisi is left). Your destination is now 3.4km up this road. A little after the Kapetanos restaurant, just before a LH bend take the RH small road down to turn sharp right over a bridge. The turning is just before an Armco barrier and after a bus shelter both on the right. It is signposted Arxontas restaurant.
Start Point	The west bank of the river before turning right over the bridge. The start of the path is effectively where the road would go if not turning right over the bridge. The route on the map starts by the Kapetanos restaurant and hence the distances on the map are from there.
Car Parking	There are a few options. There's a small layby opposite the Kapetanos restaurant and another further along heading towards Elefonisi. Car parking spaces are marked on either side of the bridge. There are also spaces on rough ground at the bridge start point. There is a car park on the right directly after going over the bridge, but you should patronise the restaurant that owns it if parking there.

Description

The walk down Topolia Gorge is quite spectacular sometimes high above the dry riverbed, sometimes crossing the riverbed itself. This walk also takes you on tracks and roads high up above the gorge for spectacular views of the entire Kissamos bay. This is one of the longer walks and you need to be comfortable with some steep paths. These only occur in a couple of places and the majority of the walk is straightforward and well worth the effort. Treat yourself to some well-earned refreshments or more, at either of the very nice and friendly restaurants at the start.

Walk Directions

1) Walk down the wide track along the west riverbank. It is easy going at first with blue markers indicating the route. It needs to be explained that the path suffered bad erosion in the storms of 2018. In places, the path fades into the riverbank only to appear again later on. Pick your route as best you can sometimes on the riverbed and sometimes on the path.

3) Topolia gorge where the path comes down to the riverbed

2) After a while, the path will disappear completely, continue by bounding over the rocks. Just as this starts to become more difficult with larger rocks to clamber over. There is a route up the west (left) bank that restores the route back to the path. This occurs just before a part with a particularly difficult drop from a rock to continue along the riverbed. The route up climbs 4-5m towards a telegraph pole and is located just past the Agia Sophia cave on the map or GPS (you cannot see it from the gorge) and meets a route down from the road. If you are not sure any route up, roughly in this location will bring you to the path. The path was

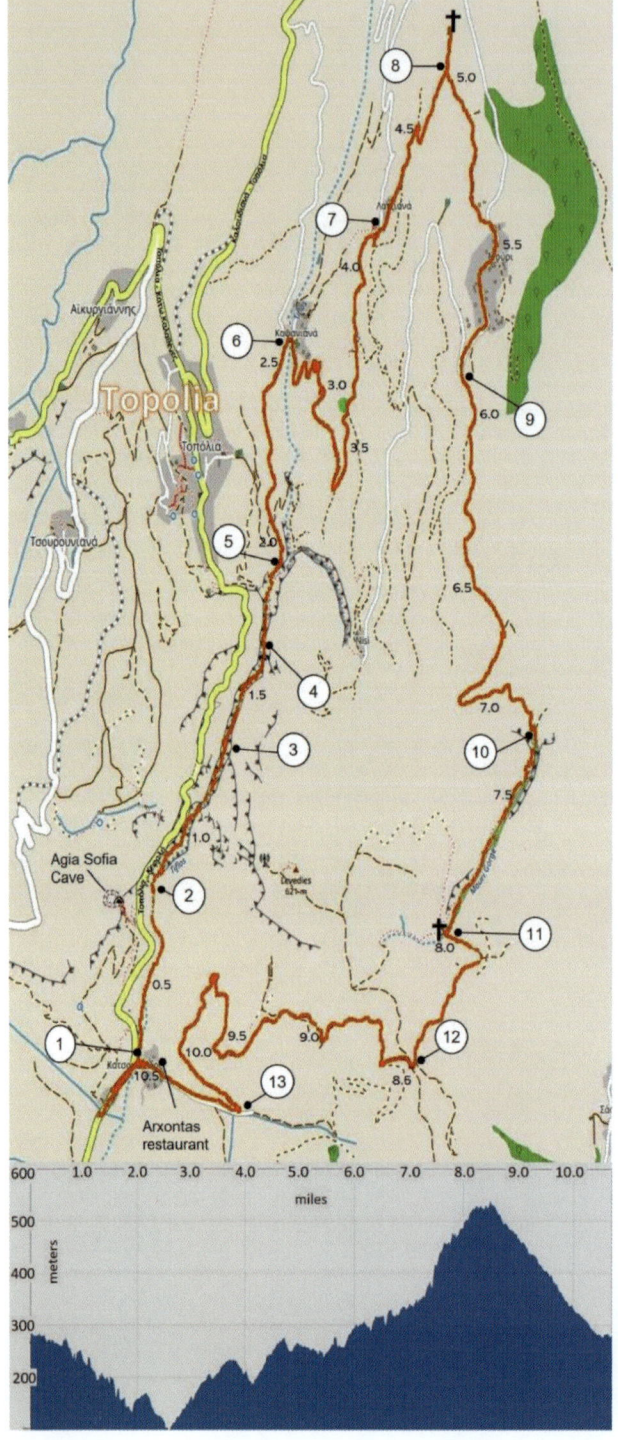

being repaired whilst we were there in 2020 so the route will be clearer in the future. Re-gain the path and continue alongside the riverbed. The route is quite clear now, enjoy the views.

3)   The path descends and eventually comes down beside the riverbed. Continue along the LH side of the river. After about 1km from originally climbing up to the path, cross the riverbed where there is a concrete causeway. Continue on the other (east) side of the riverbed.

4)   Some small caves appear at the bottom of the rock face. When you see the larger one on the west bank cross over and continue the walk on that (left) side.

5)   Our route leaves the path beside the riverbed and continues on tracks and roads. The exiting track starts by passing through a fence to the left of a large square concrete waterworks structure to the left of the riverbed. It is also where the riverbed is populated with trees and it is difficult to continue that way. Climb the track to a Y junction, take the LH fork continuing upwards. At the next junction turn right. After the junction, the track remains roughly straight heading northwards and descending along the side of the valley to Kapsaniana village, with great views to the other side of the valley, where we are going next.

6)   On reaching the tarmac road at the village turn right to immediately cross a bridge and then turn right again. The road now initially zig-zags up the hillside becoming a gravel track before heading southwards but still climbing and turning, you can see straight across to the village of Topolina on the other

side of the valley. At a sharp 180-degree LH hairpin bend, the route starts to head north again. Follow the contour of the hillside to the next village, Datziana.

7) Datziana starts where the gravel track finishes at a junction with a tarmac road on a bend. There is a nice meeting area on the RH side of the road with a long bench and a tap under shady trees, no doubt for visitors to the church below the track on the LH side. Below the church are the ruins of another earlier church which is worth a look. At the junction turn right up a tarmac road and climb out of the village. Carry straight on and the route zig-zags up the hillside to head north again. Before that, there is turning up the hill on the right that can be mistaken for the zig-zag but takes you off the main track (this is not shown on the map).

8) The route comes to a T junction with a sign pointing right to the village Moypi, 700m. Our route is to turn left instead, going to the church Aghios Antonios and return to this point. The church is worth a visit to sit on the benches and take in the magnificent view of the Kissamos bay and the villages below, probably the highlight of the walk. After visiting the church return the way you came to pass the original junction heading straight on. Follow the track down to a junction and turn right along the tarmac road to walk through the village of Moypi.

Kissamos bay vista at Aghios Antonios Church

9) After leaving the village take the track straight ahead off the road on a 180-degree RH hairpin bend. After 250m take the LH fork at a Y junction. The RH fork going up the hill and your LH fork staying more or less level. Stay on this track following the contours of the hillside.

10) Pass around a large RH 180-degree bend and the track twists and turns before arriving at a 180 LH bend at the bottom of a gorge (map only shows a small part of the continuing track). Leave the track here to take the path up through the Mouri gorge. The path is not that clear, there was a small blue wooden sign saying "Ar Athanasios" which is the church at the top. There are blue dots marking the route which are reasonably reliable. Either way with all the goat tracks pick the best route you can to the top mainly to the left of the riverbed (but not always).

11) At the top of the gorge keep go straight on as the route levels out to meet a gravel track coming from the church on the RH side. Turn left along the track. Further up, at a junction on a bend turn right up the hill.

12) After a climb, the route levels out before rising again up to a complex junction behind a fence-gate. Ignore the LH turn just before the gate. Pass through the gate turning right and then immediately take the descending LH fork heading downwards as opposed to the ascending RH fork. Initially make your way down to a RH hairpin bend and turn right. The route is now a clear wide track all the way. Ignore side turnings and stay with the main track winding and descending.

13) The track brings you down to the bottom of a gorge where you cross the riverbed turning right to now head straight back to the start. Treat yourself to some well-earned refreshments or more, at either of the very nice and friendly restaurants.

8. Ferries
Q. Agia Roumeli Lower West Fort

Distance	2.8 miles, 4.4 km.
Ascent	291m, 955 ft
How to Get There	Take the ferry from Paleochora. There is no road route to Agia Roumeli
Start Point	At the ferry jetty

Description

Views along the coast from lower west fort

Agia Roumeli is the endpoint for all the walkers who complete the ever-popular Samaria Gorge. It can only be reached by ferry or on foot and the ferries are kept very busy in the afternoon taking walkers back to coaches at either Sougia in the west or Loutro in the east. It is quite an amusing bedraggled parade, with lyrca clad fitness enthusiasts amongst struggling people of all shapes, age and sizes.

This short walk takes you up to the old, ruined Lower West Fort above the town for excellent panoramic views to the coast and down to the end of the Samaria gorge. Although it is short in distance the climb up to the fort is very steep on loose stone surfaces. In places, it's about as steep as you can get without the need to employ hands. It is quite safe if you are cautious but those who suffer vertigo will not enjoy it. In hot weather it can be exhausting, lots of water is needed, do not underestimate the effort required based on the length and assent. The return route from the fort is a lot easier and quite welcome after the steep climb up. You may like to venture to the second fort, although it is known that others have visited it we have not and cannot vouch for the route personally.

Walk Directions
1)   When leaving the ferry keep to the stone wall on the LH side and walk into the town. At the first junction with a car park on the right, turn right through the shops and bars. Then, at the next junction turn left and head up to the road at the back of the town to turn right, heading out of town past some more restaurants.

2)   The large metal gates of a church on the left come into view behind a continuous wire fence on the LH side. Pass the church and just afterwards find the gate in the fence to a path which is the start of the climb up to the fort. Pass through the gate and climb the rough zig-zag path lined with low stone walls.

3)   The stone walls soon run out and the path becomes quite indistinct red stone and dust. Keep heading upwards following the route that looks most used. There is much zig-zagging and it is very steep. If the direction you are taking starts to look implausible stop and look around there is normally an easier option amongst the many difficult ones taken by those who don't mind a scramble.

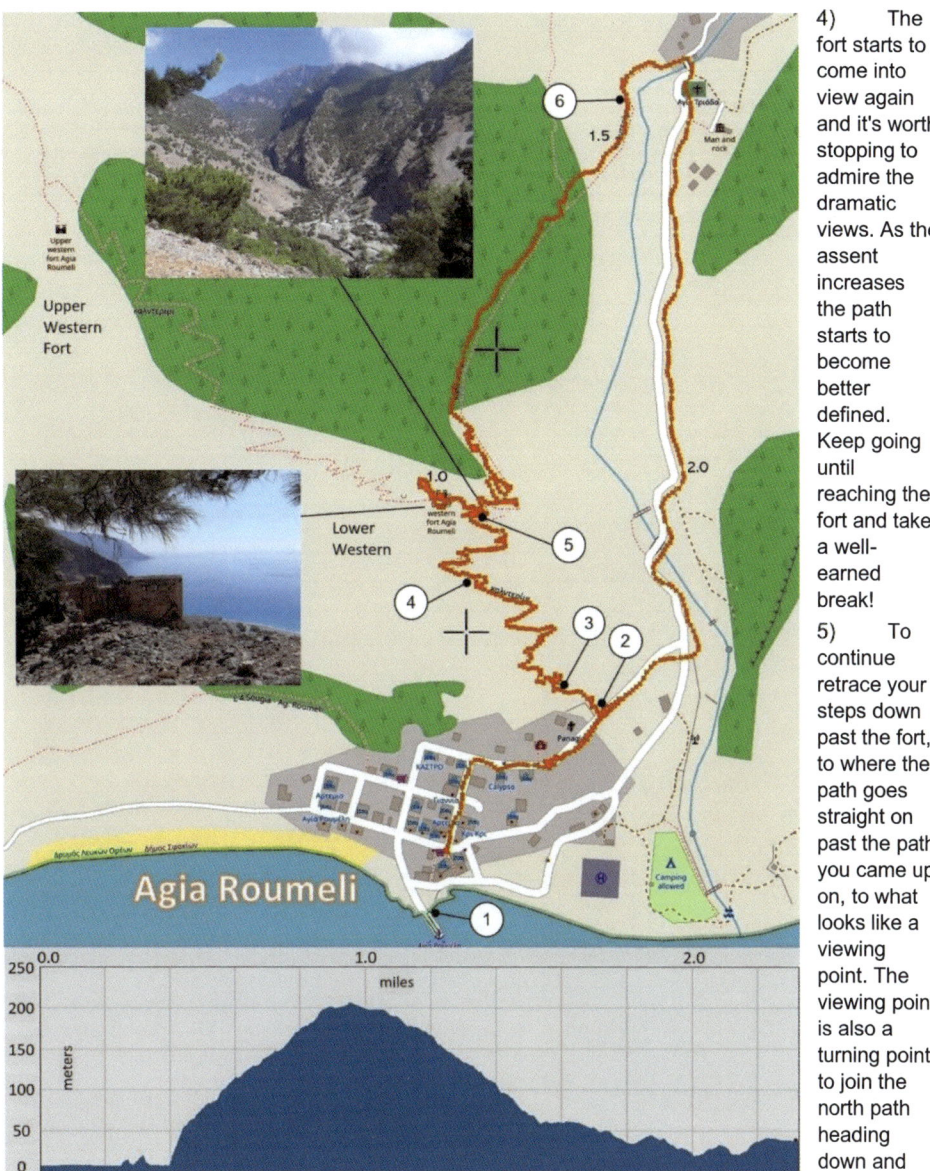

4) The fort starts to come into view again and it's worth stopping to admire the dramatic views. As the assent increases the path starts to become better defined. Keep going until reaching the fort and take a well-earned break!

5) To continue retrace your steps down past the fort, to where the path goes straight on past the path you came up on, to what looks like a viewing point. The viewing point is also a turning point to join the north path heading down and along the hillside. The start of the route and the route itself is marked with red painted symbols similar to the old Campaign for Nuclear Disarmament (CND) symbols. In contrast to the path up this path is well constructed and easy to follow.

6) Eventually, after passing another route on the left the path approaches the riverbed. Where there is a wire fence meeting the path on the left take the route down to the dry part of the riverbed, not following the fence line as some have done. The path rises again to the base of a large stone wall. Follow the wall around to the right and go over the stone bridge to reach the main gorge road. Turn right to head back into town.

R. Sougia Circular

Distance	3.7 miles, 6km
Ascent	287m, 942ft
How to Get There	Travel by ferry from Paleochora (or Agia Roumeli) or by car
Start Point	The centre of Sougia on the coast road. Or the ferry Jetty
Car Parking	Car parks can be found on the left of the main Sougia coast/beach road at the ferry end (west) and at the east end of the beach road If parked in the western end car park, start at point 2.

Description

If you want to combine a ferry trip along the dramatic coastline, past the Crocodile, towering cliffs and picture-postcard fishing villages and a short walk, this is ideal. The walk takes you through a spectacular rock cleft and wooded areas up to a peak with good coastal views. Sougia town is a pleasant place to spend some time while you await your ferry home with lots of restaurants and bars and a laid back atmosphere.

Walk Directions

Spectacular rock cleft

1) Walk west along the coast road to the ferry jetty and go to the right of the ticket booth at the end, carrying straight on along the road. Pass the small harbour on the left, following the road curving around the harbour.

2) The road ends with the start of the gorge on the right with a map board on the left of the entrance. Follow the path up the gorge.

3) After 20minutes or so climb down into a spectacular rock cleft in the gorge that reaches high overhead. Continue to follow the path up through a wooded area.

4) The route arrives at a path going left up the side of the gorge signposted Lissos on a tree. Do not take this route but keep travelling straight on.

5) Following the path through the trees, look for a red marker at the base of a tree in the middle of the path. It is here that the route climbs up right, out of the gorge. The path climbs steeply up through the rocks at first and becomes a pleasant climbing path after a while through the woods, marked with red dots.

6) After a short while, the highest point is reached with the path levelling off with a dip in terrain ahead.

7) The route peaks again before descending in earnest.

8) Keep following the path with good views to the coast appearing during the descent with the White mountains in the background.

5) Red paint indicates where to leave the gorge

WARNING: Be careful not to deviate from the path because there are some large, unmarked sinkholes just off the route.

9) Sougia town will come into view further on over the edge of the path.
10) The path becomes a rough wide gravel track descending quite steeply and care needs to be taken because of the large loose stones.
11) Keep zig-zagging down the path until joining the road below. Take a sharp right back to Sougia.

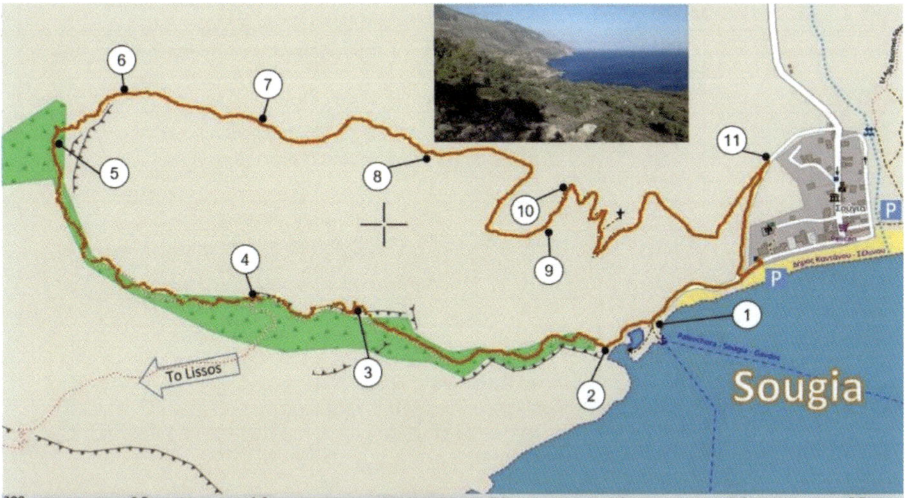

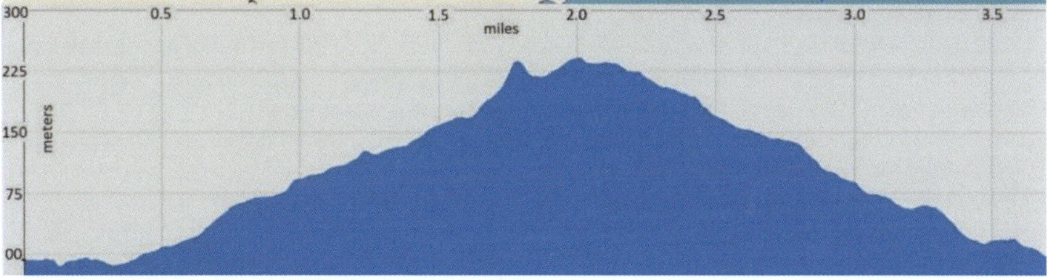

9) Sougia comes into view before the descent

S. Sougia, Polyphemos Cave (Adventurous)

Distance	6.4 miles, 10.3km
Ascent	520m, 1703ft
How to Get There	Travel by ferry from Paleochora (or Agia Roumeli) or by car
Start Point	Form the ferry landing point, or centre of Sougia/ Sougia Car Park
Car Parking	Can be found on the left of the main Sougia coast/beach road up to the ferry (west) and at the east end of the beach road (the other direction to the ferry).

Description

The shorter of two walks that visit the Cave of Polyphemos. We're calling this adventurous because there is a climb up a hillside with no defined path. The climb up to a rocky ridge through scrubland and trees with great views, sometimes of Gavdos island, but the highlight of the walk is the visit to the Cave of Polyphemus. Legend has it that the giant one-eyed cannibal Cyclops captured Odysseus and his companions. After plying him with wine and blinding him with a burning stake, Odysseus and his companions escaped from the cave disguised by wearing sheep fleeces and hiding with the sheep let out each morning. Although it has a small entrance the cave is large inside with impressive rock formations. Once you have visited the cave you wind your way back to Sougia along the E4 footpath for some refreshments at the many bars and cafes.

Walk Directions

1) Walk up the main road out of Sougia, keep going until you are at the last set of apartments on the right, Idomeneas apartments. At the end of the apartments where the wall ends take the turning right on a gravel road. Pass a road meeting you from the right and cross the dry storm river. At the other side follow the gravel road uphill heading northeast with a high chain-link fence on the left.

2) After a left and RH bend, the road becomes concrete. Stay on this road, twisting and turning up the hill Ignore turnings off to the left. There are good views back to Sougia.

3) You will pass a reconstructed traditional village with round stone buildings on the right. We do not know the motivation behind this village, why or for what it has been constructed. It does not look occupied, but it is quite impressive and clearly a fair amount of money has been thrown at it. Carry on and the road becomes gravel again.

4) At a T junction with another gravel road turn right following the contour of the hill south, with a slight descent. There is a fence on the right, look for a goat path up to the left behind two trees after the fence has finished (pictured).

5) This is where the fun starts; there is not a consistent path up the hillside, the method is to scramble up twisting and turning as best suits the terrain. The path behind the trees initially heads southwest for a little way, after that, the path is unclear, but change direction east heading directly up towards the saddle on the ridge between two outcrops of rock. Our route took us through the gap between a small rock set apart on the

left of a larger formation of rocks on the right. The slope surface is quite loose but there is sufficient gradient that a slip would result in a short slide and not a fall, in this way it is reasonably safe.

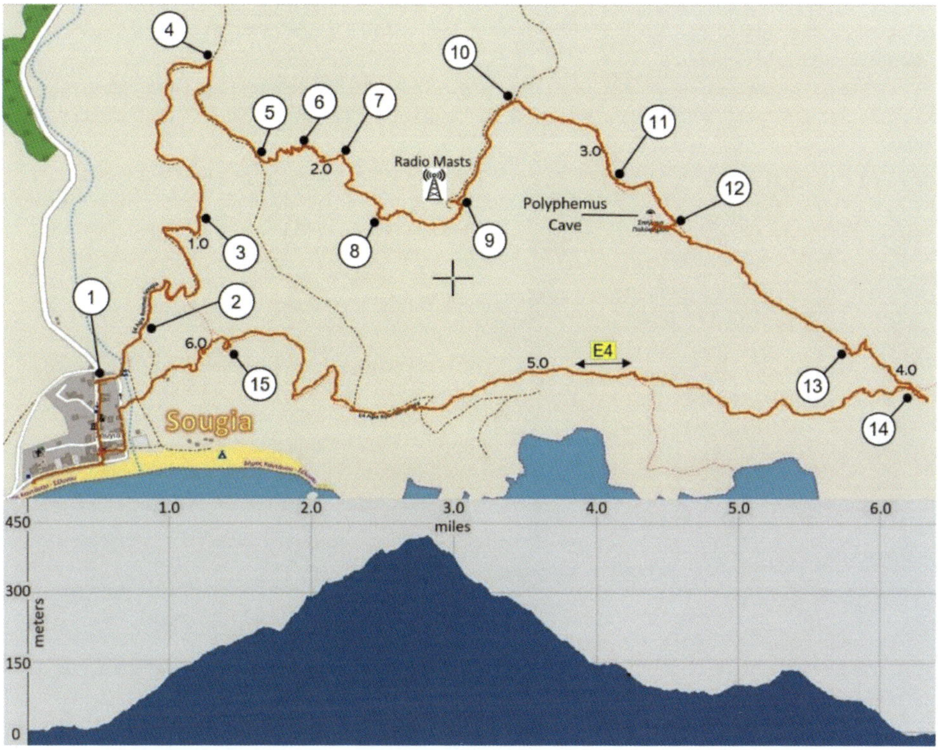

6) On reaching the top of the ridge there is an open area with grass and trees the other side, drop down and go to the right across the level ground heading southeast into the trees on the other side, climb up the bank heading east through the trees.

Approach radio mast on the right

7) Exit the trees to find clear rocky ground with some scrub. Now head roughly southeast again, climbing steadily along the side of a depression to the left. Make your way to the higher ground on your right and keep heading southeast.

8) You are heading to approach the RH side of the radio mast above, however, the direct route is steep and difficult. Keep heading roughly southeast and circulate without too much difficulty, around the RH side of the rocky outcrop rising in front of you. Once clear of the steepest rocks pick your way up to the left and make your way ascending the open terrain to the radio mast.

9) At the radio mast enjoy the splendid views, and with the most difficult part of the walk over a sense of achievement. The route now follows the concrete service road north.

10) Some 400m meters along the concrete road there is a path on the right leading to Polyphemus' cave. The path is marked with sometimes blue and sometimes blue and white paint. You are helped

finding the start of the path because it is opposite a gravel track (not on the map) going left from the concrete road and easier to locate. Leave the concrete road turning off right and follow the makers across the rocky scrub land rising at first and then descending. As the route starts to descend, look for a lone tree to the right of others with a metal pipe on the right of it. Pass to the right of the tree and keep following the blue makers.

11) After passing a cavernous gully hidden behind the trees on the left the path veers left to pass over the end of the gully. After which, still following the markers, turn right down the hill through the trees.

12) look for a clear sign to the cave on a tree to the right of the path, at head height, pointing right. Follow the path, confused with use, from the tree, turning right around the rocks at the end to find Polyphemos' cave. After exploring the cave return to the main path and continue the descent, again following the blue and white markers.

13) When you see a white stone cross on a concrete plinth on a headland you are coming near to the end of the descent, keep following the blue and white markers. The path turns sharp right and then left here to help negotiate the steeper descent.

14) The descent reaches the E4 coastal path crossing

View of the entrances from inside the cave

east-west in a shady area amongst trees to the right of a shallow valley. Join the E4 at an acute angle, turning sharp right to join it. There is a sign on one of the trees pointing west marked Sougia indicating the way back. Follow the E4 route back to Sougia, with great views along the coast.

15) When approaching down into Sougia there are several options for paths. The route shown seemed the most direct and is marked with an E4 flag. It turns off sharp left after a 180-degree 'U' bend (looks like a loop on the map) from the main wide gravel road and zig-zags down. Any route that takes you to and across the wide storm river will bring you back to the start.

T. Sougia, Polyphemos Cave

Distance	9.7 miles, 15.6 km
Ascent	680m, 2231ft
How to Get There	Travel by ferry from Paleochora (or Agia Roumeli) or by car
Start Point	The centre of Sougia on the coast road. Or the ferry jetty
Car Parking	Car parks can be found on the left of the main Sougia coast/beach road up to the ferry (west) and at the east end of the beach road (the other direction to the ferry). If parked in the eastern car park start at point 2.

Description

Polyphemos?

The longer and more strenuous walk to the Cave of Polyphemos in this book, so make sure you allow time to catch the ferry back, unless you have driven there by car. The walk is part of the main E4 footpath and is well signposted. See Walk S for the legend of the cave. The walk zig-zags up a hill, with great panoramas along the coastline to the east and the west. After visiting the cave you climb again up a ridge to the village of Koustogerako with its pleasant small plaza and war memorial, then down a twisty track past the ruined village of Livados in the distance zig-zagging your way along tracks and roads back to Sougia where you can enjoy a rest at one of the many beachside restaurants.

Walk Directions

1) From the ferry jetty start by walking east from the ferry ramp into Sougia. Pass by all the restaurants with their covered beachside tables and pass the main road out of Sougia on the left. Keep going to the end of the road and turn left at the end where it becomes a gravel track along the side of the wide storm channel coming out of Irini gorge. Head up this track along the back of the shops. NB: You will start from here if parked in the eastern car park.

2)   Just over about halfway up this road find a rough route heading diagonally across the storm channel heading roughly northeast. The route leads off the track opposite the Polyfimus restaurant. Crossing to the other side of the channel and the bushes there, look for some wooden signs to Polyfimus/Poliphimos Cave (and other such spellings). Follow these where they exist.

3)   Keep heading through the bushes on the rough tracks, looking for a sturdy galvanised fence around the perimeter of some buildings, continue down a track on the LH side of this fence. The fence leads to a stone wall, continue with the route along the side of the wall. Follow the path as it climbs up through a wooded area and becomes a single track and then zig-zags up a bank before continuing east in the same direction.

4) As the path starts to level off you reach the E4 route at a T junction. The E4 at this point is much wider (sufficient for 4x4 vehicles and you can't miss it). At the junction looking left is the way you return. Turn right along the track, which bears right followed by an immediate 180-degrees LH

bend up the hill, there are yellow and black E4 paint markers on the rocks and trees to guide us.

5) The track stays wide with large zig-zags up the hill, keep following the route up to the crest. Another track from the left as the summit approaches. Ahead in the distance can be seen four outcrops of land reaching further out into the sea. We are heading to the depression between the first and the second where the route leaves the E4 heading northeast up to the cave.

6) Stay on the marked E4 track. At the start of the descent from the crest there is a chain across the track. Step over the chain and take the narrow path to the right. This path shortcuts the route of the main track. There are great panoramas along the coast to the east and the west from here. Keep following the single track path across the hillside.

7) After about 0.6 of a mile and a 90 degree RH turn there is a stone threshing circle just off the main path to the right. This a good place for a rest to enjoy the view. Afterwards keep following the E4 path around the hillside and down into the depression between the two hills.

8) As the E4 then starts to climb a little out of the depression under the trees the path to the cave is up in front of you going to the left at an acute angle to the E4 direction. It is not that clear at first but there is a sign on a tree above on the hillside to the left indicating the direction. The cave is half a mile from this junction. There are now blue and white paint markers to follow and the going can become quite steep.

9) The path arrives at a gully, cross this and climb steeply out of the gully on the other side to turn right and continue up the hill.
10) After half a mile from leaving the E4, amongst some trees, there is a small path heading off slightly downhill to the left and around the hillside. This is the route to the cave. If you miss it look around for a sign on a tree to the left of our route up the hill only directly visible to walkers descending the hill (because it's on the wrong side of the tree for us, pictured in walk S). Follow the path towards the edge of the hill and then a little way around to the right to find the cave entrances; there are two of them on either side of a boulder. It is a little underwhelming from the outside, but the interior

The RH cave entrance

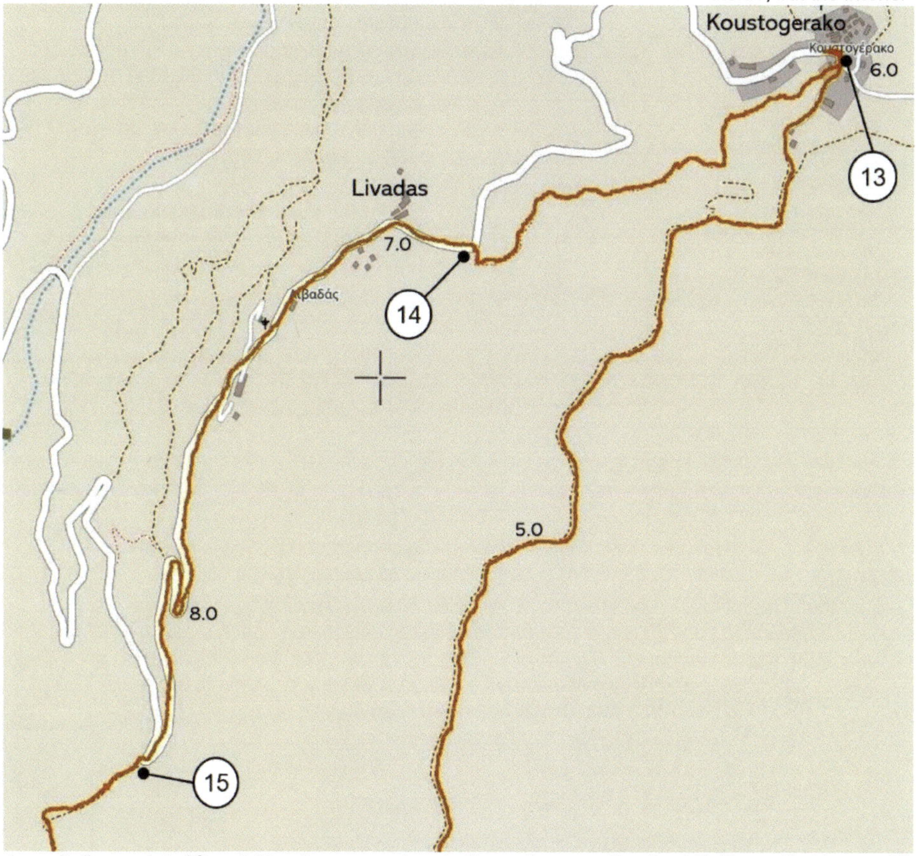

doesn't disappoint. After visiting the cave return to the path ascending the hill. Keep climbing up. The path can be a little unclear in places, but the blue and white markers can still be seen here and there.

11) The route turns left around a very deep gully before heading north again. Keep heading up the hillside. If you lose the markers, you may pick your own route, it is not an issue; keep approaching and then cross ridge above before descending to meet a wide gravel track crossing east to west, i.e. just keep going until you meet the track.

12) At the gravel track turn right to the village of Koustogerako, (the route left, goes to the radio masts where there are excellent views down to the coast should you have the inclination). Simply stay on the track into the village. It twists and turns, ascends and descends, stay on it until reaching the village.

The Memorial at Koustogerako

13) At the village the track meets a road at a T junction. Turn left and notice immediately on the left a house with a path down the LH side, this is our return route to Sougia. I suggest first passing the house to find a small square on the left with benches and a statue of a partisan representing those who fought and died against the Nazis. This is a good spot to take a break should you desire. Afterwards, take the path down the side of the house and notice a stone memorial on the right on the other side of the fence. Keep following this small path descending slowly along the side of the hill. You are walking down to the road below. The road is getting close when the interesting ruins of the village Livadas comes into view on a lower hill up ahead on the right, about half a mile from Koustogerako.

14) Following the path, join the road by descending a steep bank onto the road surface. Continue down the road (left) now for 1 mile. You will come to a long zig-zag with the road first turning 180-degrees to the right and then the left. We looked for a shortcut down here but couldn't find one, good luck if you do.

15) After the zig-zag approach another 180-degree right turn for the road, there is a gravel track going straight ahead on the bend, take this climbing uphill. The climb ends with a 90 degree LH bend after which the descent starts.

16) Just before a long RH bend ignore the track turning off to the left. Although this is an alternative if you should choose it. Our route heads right following the bend around the hillside. Stay on this main track making your way back to Sougia.

17) After about 700m from turning off the road, on a straight part of the track to your left, you will come across an interesting rebuilt traditional village, similar to the buildings at Milia.

18) After the village and a LH bend our route turns left on a RH bend off the main track. You can also remain on the main track (it is a proper track incorrectly designated as a footpath on the map) to arrive back to the storm channel and back to Sougia. However, we took the LH track which goes back to the junction where we joined the E4 at the start. Make your way back to Sougia either way and enjoy a rest there at the beachside restaurants before your ferry.

U. Sougia to Paleochora

Distance	10.2 miles, 16.4 km.
Ascent	554m, 1818ft
How to Get There	Travel to Sougia by ferry from Paleochora (or Agia Roumeli) or by car (but the walk is linear), or bus.
Start Point	The centre of Sougia on the coast road. Or the ferry jetty.
Car Parking	Car parks can be found on the left of the main Sougia coast/beach road up to the ferry (west) and at the east end of the beach road (the other direction to the ferry).

Description

One of the best and most popular walks due to the opportunity to explore the tranquil ancient ruins of Lissos. You start with a ferry journey to Sougia, and although it is a long walk you encounter two beaches, a secluded bay where you can rest and swim with a great café/bar before finishing with a scenic (but dusty) walk along the coast to Paleochora. Lissos has been dated back to ancient Crete. In 1957–58 the city was excavated by N. Platon who discovered ruins of a theatre, aqueduct, cemetery and baths of the ancient times, and Paleo-Christian basilicas. Many people do the walk in reverse i.e. Paleochora to Sougia but going west to east means you must time your walk to catch the ferry at Sougia to return, which may not be a problem if you don't mind rising relatively early. Going east to west does mean you can take all the time to want to explore Lissos and enjoy the Gialiskari beach at the bottom of the Anidri gorge.

The route is the signposted E4 coastal route, but this walk gives you an option to deviate and explore the many Roman tombs in the western hillside of Lissos bay. With its high cliffs, this coastal route seems to attract the heat from the sun so do not underestimate the effort and the amount of water you will need.

Walk Directions

1) Walk west along the coast road to the ferry jetty and go to the right of the ticket booth at the end, carrying straight on along the road. Pass the small harbour on the left. Keep following the road curving around the harbour to the right. The road ends at the start of the gorge with a map board on the left of the route. Simply keep following the path up the gorge.

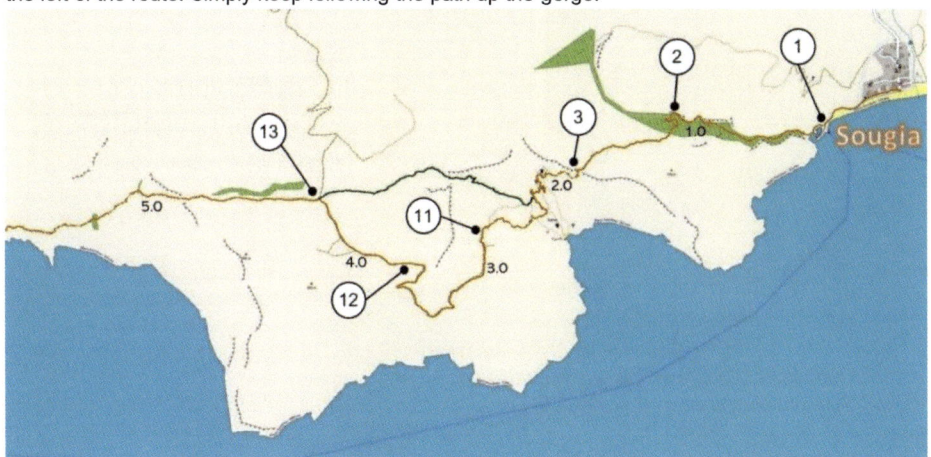

2) After 20 minutes or so climb down into a spectacular rock cleft in the gorge that reaches high above overhead. Continuing, follow the path up through a wooded area. The path to leave the gorge

is on the left, signposted Lissos on a tree. Turn left and climb the initially well-made path supported on stone walls up through the pine trees to the treeless plateau at the top. When at the top keep following the path westwards across the plateau to the edge of the Lissos valley.

3)   At the edge of the valley take time to admire the view from here, take in the general layout of this ancient tranquil location to get your bearings. The Roman necropolis tombs are straight across on the other side with the bay coastline to the south. The E4 rises out of the valley to the right of the tombs. Descend into the valley using the path built into the steep hillside.

Lissos Valley

Asclepius Temple

4)   Following the route down the hills side to finish the descent with the fenced-off ruins of the 3rd century BC Asclepius Temple on the right. At the front of the fenced off area is a gate which allows access to the temple. There is a mosaic floor that not long ago, before the fence, was open for goats to freely wander across. From the temple keep heading straight ahead (west) to the church of Agios Kyrikos which has some nice frescoes.

5)   Visit the church and then head south to a picnic area with flowing fresh water, a good place to take a rest. If you should like to explore the rest of the valley and the beach, it is a good idea to do so from here and then return to this spot to continue. Further down towards the beach of the LH side is the chapel of Panagia built with ancient marble blocks from the valley.

6)   From the picnic spot head west to find some arched tombs. Pass them on the left and come across the ruins of a large square stone building. Following the route now head south past the left of the building. This is the E4 route to Paelochora (green on the map) it is signposted off to the right.

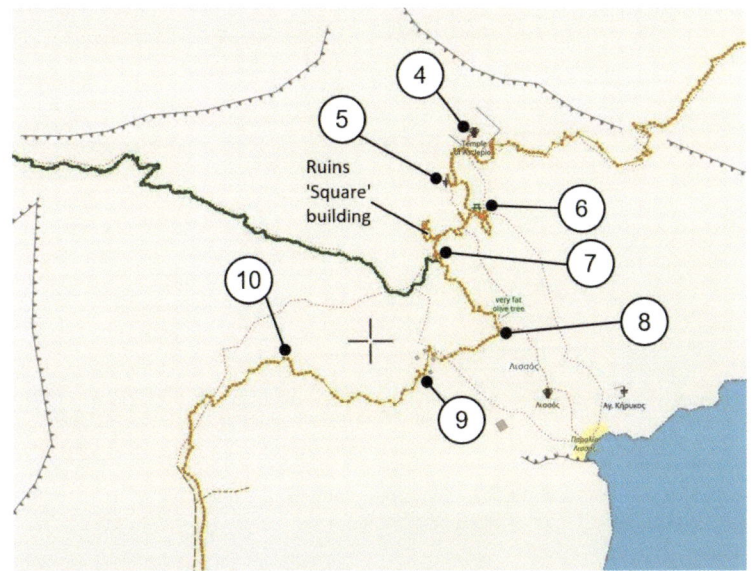

Take the E4 if you don't want to visit the tombs on the west valley side, which adds about half a mile, but the ascent is slightly less although arguably more difficult. I will only describe the route via the tombs because the E4 route is marked and straightforward to follow. One reason for not visiting the tombs is that a small part of the route up from the tombs to a clear track is hard to follow and describe. If you are not comfortable with this you could go up to the tombs and retrace your steps, or simply miss them out altogether and remain on the E4. My route up to the tombs is only one way of getting there and it is open territory with many alternative and viable options.

7)   Just pass the 'square building' where the E4 turns right, leave the E4 and head down (south) across the terraces, to a low terrace wall with a large (relatively) open area on the other side.

8)   At the terrace wall turn right following roughly the course of the wall and head up into the tomb area. Keep going up the hill and climb in amongst the tombs.

Lissos Tombs

9) There's lots to explore in the tomb area, it's estimated that there are about 50, so take your time and enjoy. There are great views back across the valley. To continue, keep heading upwards until almost past the tombs and the going forward becomes difficult. Keep above the cleft on your left. Now head northeast cross country using rough paths, keeping the ridge above you on the left. Look for a small path running northeast to southwest. It is not the red dotted path shown on the map, although it does merge with that later.

10)   On reaching the northeast to southwest narrow path, turn left and follow it uphill. The path leads out onto a wide gravel track, turn left here along the track.

11)   Follow the main wide gravel track. First travelling south then following the curve of the hill to head north, ascending all the way.

12) The final climb up from the coast is a rough zig-zag up the hillside first turning right and then left, after which the highest point is reached with a view down to a plateau and the back of the 'crocodile' on the left. Continue on the track descend down and across the plateau to a clear crossroads with the E4.

Passing over the Crocodile

13) At the crossroads turn left and follow the track past the back of the crocodile head after which the track narrows to a path and the descent begins in earnest. This route is very popular and easy to follow, plus there are the E4 yellow and black markers here and there. I think parts of this route, with the hillside falling into the clear blue of the Mediterranean is some of the most picturesque walking in Crete.

14) When the main descent comes to an end Astropelekita beach can be seen down on the shoreline, you can take a short detour here to enjoy the water and cool down at this normally secluded small bay. Back on the E4, the route becomes an up and down track slowly making its way to the rocks above the shore. The yellow and black route markers are still prevalent. Stay on the path to reach Andri beach, or Gialiskari beach to give it its official name, where there are refreshments at the bar/cafe and surprisingly good toilets.

15) From Andri beach, the route to Paleochora is straightforward. Head west out of the car park and follow the gravel track along the coast. There is a free mini-bus sometimes for this route, ask at the café for timings. It's also often possible to hitch a lift if your party is small. At the end of the gravel track turn left at the road for it to take you into the heart of Paleochora. The gravel track is just over 1.5 miles and the road part is about a mile.

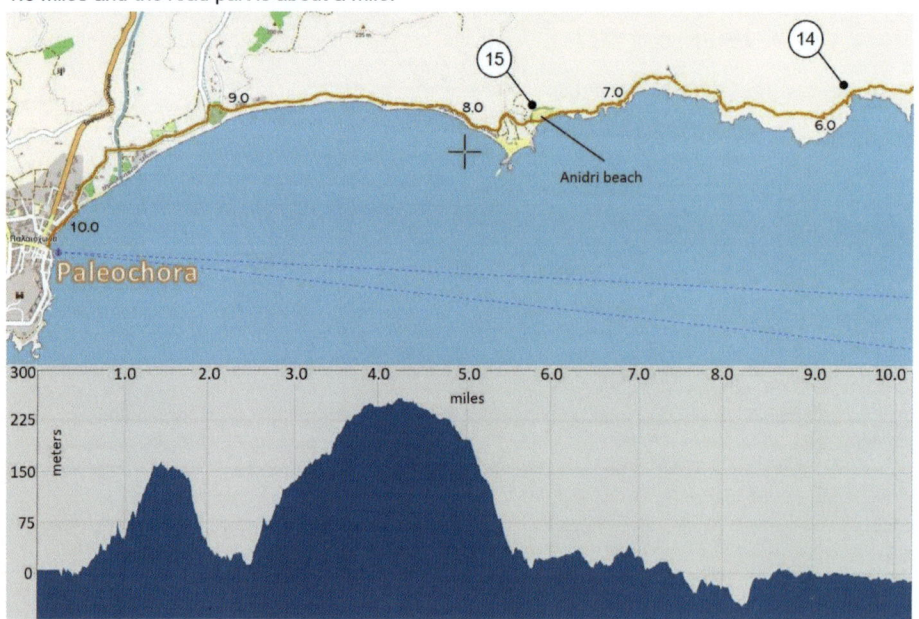

V. Elefonisi

Distance	7 miles, 11.3 km.
Ascent	257m, 843ft
How to Get There	Please see Walk H for directions. However, a taxi is best because you won't be returning to the start point if getting the ferry back from Elephonisi.
Start Point	Krios beach
Car Parking	There are parking areas at Krios beach should you be intending to walk back again from Elefonisi. The ferry will bring you back to Paleochora.

Description

Said to be one of the best beaches in the world Elefonisi is a natural lagoon that traps the crystal clear water behind sandbanks. Due to the slow-moving current, the water remains warm like a bath and is never deeper than chest height. There are beach huts serving refreshments and sunbeds with parasols.

The first couple of miles of this walk are the same as for walk H Krios Three Beaches. You can refer to that walk for more detailed information and a map of the first 2 miles. The route is the E4 route the entire way, marked with yellow and black signs and paint. Elefonisi and the Kedrodasos area are protected natural habitats which means that thankfully despite its popularity the area is largely unspoilt by human construction.

Although this is a linear one-way walk it is not unknown for more experienced walkers to walk the return route as well, which will make it 14miles or so. However, do not underestimate the energy-sapping effort of walking through several miles of sand and loose shingle along the shoreline. Take plenty of water.

Elefonisi Ferry

Operates every day except Sunday. It leaves Paleochora at 9 am and returns from Elefonisi at 4 pm. These times are changeable, check. It is not unknown for the ferry not to turn up in the afternoon to bring passengers back from Elefonisi because the sea is too choppy. It is worth considering doing the walk in reverse (Elefonisi to Krios) so you are not dependant on the ferry and you can take your time at the beach and the many shoreline alcoves on the way back. A taxi from Paleochora will pick you up from Krios but make sure you have their number before you leave.

Walk Directions

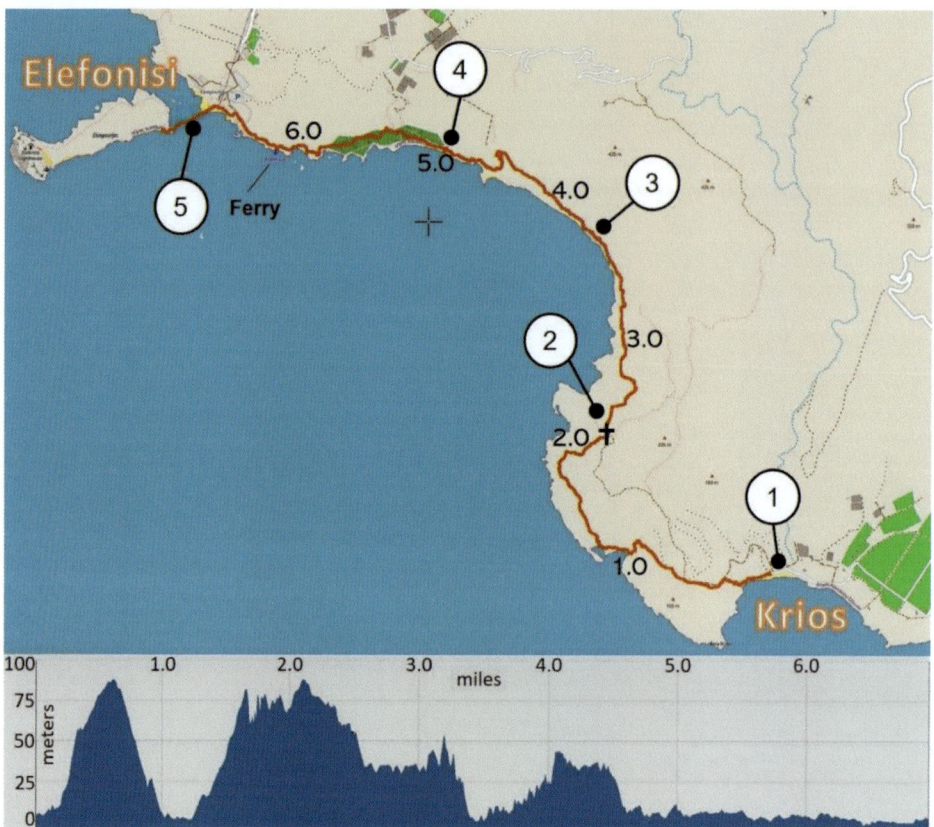

1) As for the three beaches walk H climb over the rock formation in the middle of the beach and make your way to the west end. Once there climb up out of the beach on a path that leads to a wide track at the top. Turn left along the track and further on either take the RH turning up to the ridge or take the path left down to Viena beach. Both routes bring you to Saint John's Church.

2) From the church, heading north, descend on the clear gravel path which picks a route through the low scrub bushes. You are heading to the beach in the middle of the bay that can be seen ahead.

3) The route will bring you down to Pahia Ammoutsa beach. Walk along the shore to the far end where the route climbs up to the higher ground. After the climb levels off the route arrives at a gully with trees and bushes. Walk down through the gully to the beach and then continue the route along the shore to Kedrodasos beach.

4) Walk through Kedrodasos beach to the sand dunes at the far end. Continue through the dunes where shade can be found amongst the Black Sabina trees and Juniper bushes. As you approach Elefonisi you will pass the point where the ferry arrives. It is out amongst the rocks on the shoreline

and it is best located by the cluster of potential passengers that will congregate there as 4 O'clock approaches. The jetty consists of removable planks that are reassembled from the boat on arrival.

5)   At Elefonisi it is possible to walk out on the sand barrier and through shallow water to the island. There is a small chapel at the far end of the island but be prepared to be underwhelmed should you visit it.

9.   Popular Linear Walks

These walks follow well establish linear routes and don't require the same level of direction detail as the others. They are popular, or in the case of the Samaria Gorge, very popular.

Buses and Ferries for the Gorges.

The best way from Paleochora to conduct the Samaria or Irini Gorge is to get the bus from Paleochora and return on the ferry. The bus leaves from the 'bus station' in town as early as 6:15, but it can vary throughout the year. It is the same bus for the Samaria and Irini with Irini arrived at first. The bus will stop at the large transport park at the Samaria, but you need to tell the driver that you are doing the Irini for them to stop the bus for you at the correct point.

Ferry tickets

Return tickets can be obtained from either of the two travel offices on either side of the prominent glass-fronted Vakakis Family café opposite the ferry jetty in Paleochora. Be warned that the ferry does not run if the weather is too windy. Always clearly ask and listen carefully to the helpful people in the ticket offices as to whether the ferry is running and the likelihood of it bringing you back.

W. Agia Irini Gorge

Almost as spectacular as the famous Samaria Gorge one of the main attractions of the Irini Gorge is that it is far less known or as popular as the Samaria. This means you will not share your route with as many people and mostly have the gorge to yourselves. The gorge is a deep cut in the rocks with magnificent views of the geology and the natural landscape. The route is maintained and there are several picnic areas and water stops along the way, a couple of which have toilets. The river has running water and it is crossed in many places by charming wooden bridges. Towards the end, some rocks are descended by a rustic log ladder. At 7.5km long and 500m of descent the gorge is about half the length and descent of the Samaria gorge. There are kilometre marking posts along the way to let you know how far you have travelled. It is not all descent with some ascent in a couple of places that always descend again to the riverbed.

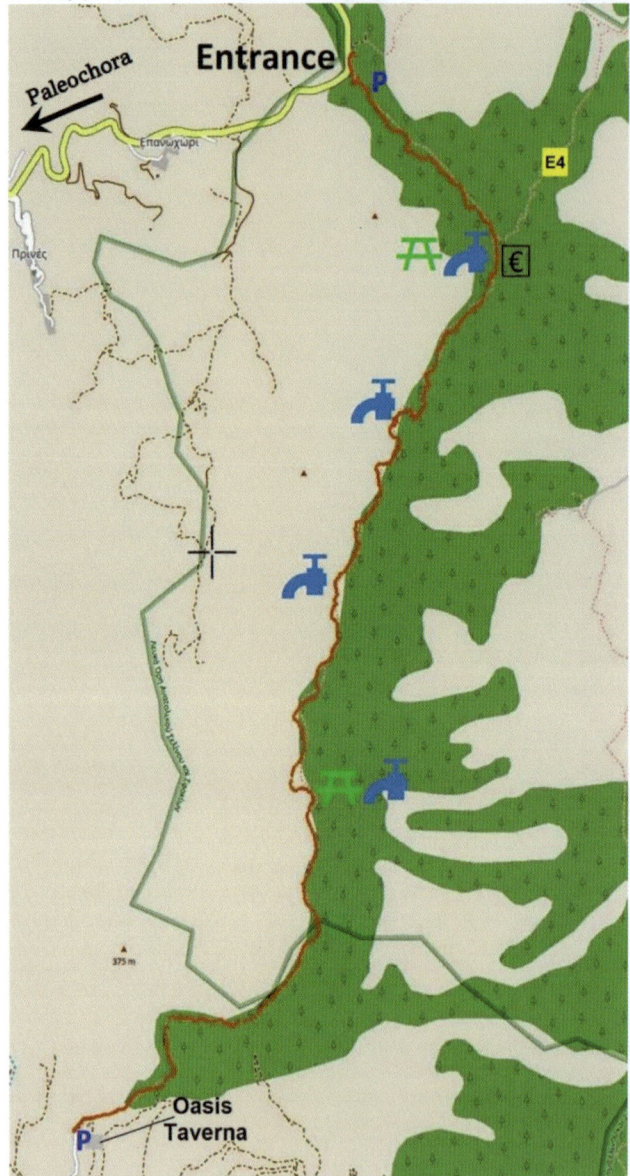

The bus stops next to Irini Gorge notices boards at the top of a concrete track which is the route to the start of the gorge. There is a small car park and a café near the entrance where you can take refreshments before your start. After about 450m the track merges with the Fughi Gorge E4 route from the left. Just past this is a stone building that houses the ticket office. It was 2 euros each when we did it.

At the end of the gorge is the Oasis Taverna open from April to October, most choose to rest here and call a taxi for the further 7km journey into Sougia. The walk into Sougia is not difficult just a bit uninspiring on tarmac, but quiet roads. However, you will have plenty of time to walk it and catch the ferry if you arrived at the start by the early morning bus. The route along the river is available to walk but it is continuously rocky which makes progress slow and hard.

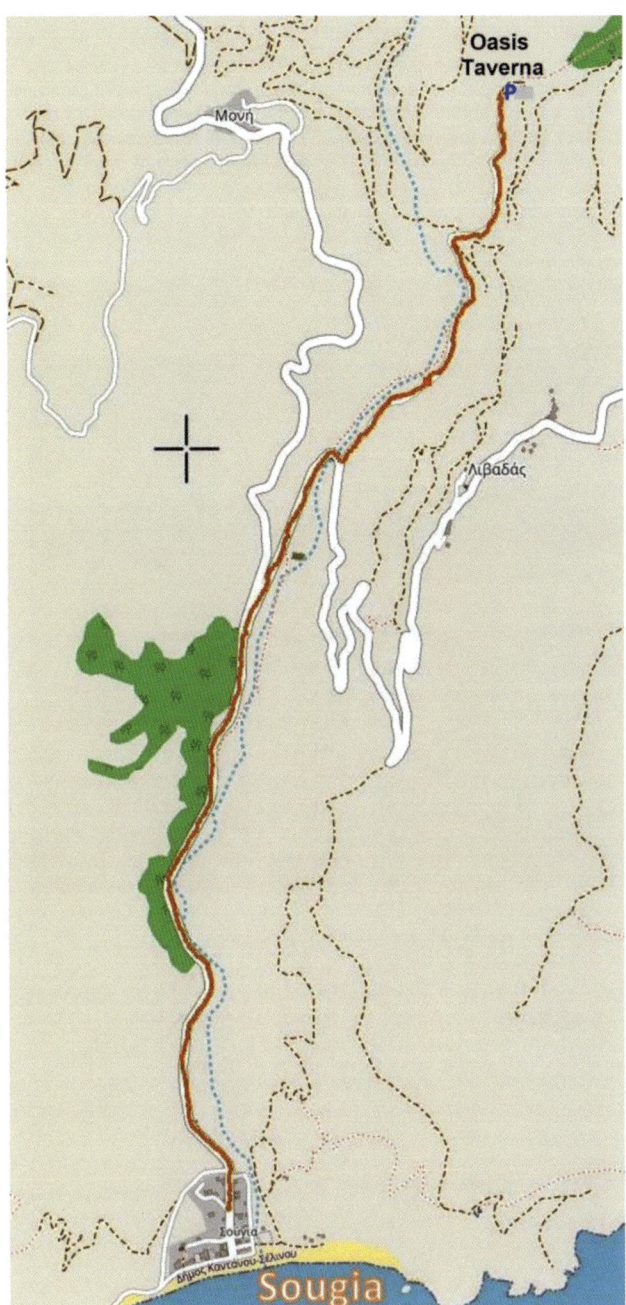

Road route into Sougia

To walk from the Oasis Taverna to Sougia, take the road south down to a junction and turn right to cross a small bridge over the river. After the bridge follow the road left and join with the main Sougia road at another junction. Continue on this road into the village to enjoy the many bars and restaurants, ice creams and a beach, whilst you wait for the ferry.

X. Samaria Gorge

The Samaria Gorge is by far the most popular and well known gorge in Crete and a must do for any keen walker. With packed coaches dropping people at the top of the gorge from all parts of the island you might think this is not your idea of a walk and being alone with nature. However, it is the longest gorge in Europe with spectacular scenery and the many and various people and cultures walking the gorge creates a kind of festival atmosphere that can be uplifting and you feel a sense of community and shared purpose. Mainly descent the whole way there is some ascent as well, but if you are reasonably fit you will enjoy this walk although it can take 5 – 7 hours with stops. Bring plenty of water and keep your bottles to fill up along the way. Wear appropriate footwear and bring some food or purchase some at the start when you get there.

The area is well maintained with the provision of dedicated water stops, picnic areas and toilets, with a self-service restaurant/café at the start. You will also see rangers keeping an eye on people and donkeys are utilised to take any injured people back to the start.

The gorge is 13km long and descends 1250m, there is a further 2km at the end of the gorge to reach the coastal village and ferry port of Agia Roumeli. The first part of the route has the steepest descent aided with provision of a rough stone pathway and wooden handrails. The gorge here is 150m at its widest, the narrowest part is only 3m at the 'Iron gates' where the cliffs are 500m above sea level. This is one of the most spectacular parts of the walk but all along you will see amazing rock formations and perhaps some of the rare and endangered Kri-kri wild goat (you may see these standing in trees), birdlife includes the bearded, Griffon Vultures and Bonelli's Eagle.

In many parts, there are wooden boardwalks over the river and along the way you will pass the ruins of Samaria village, which was abandoned in 1962 to make way for the Samaria National Park which is itself part of Crete's White Mountain National Park.

You even get brave souls walking up the Gorge to stay the night in lodgings on the Omalos plateau, but most start at the top, walk down, catch the ferry to Sougia (west) or Loutro (east) to board coaches and return, tired but happy from whence they came.

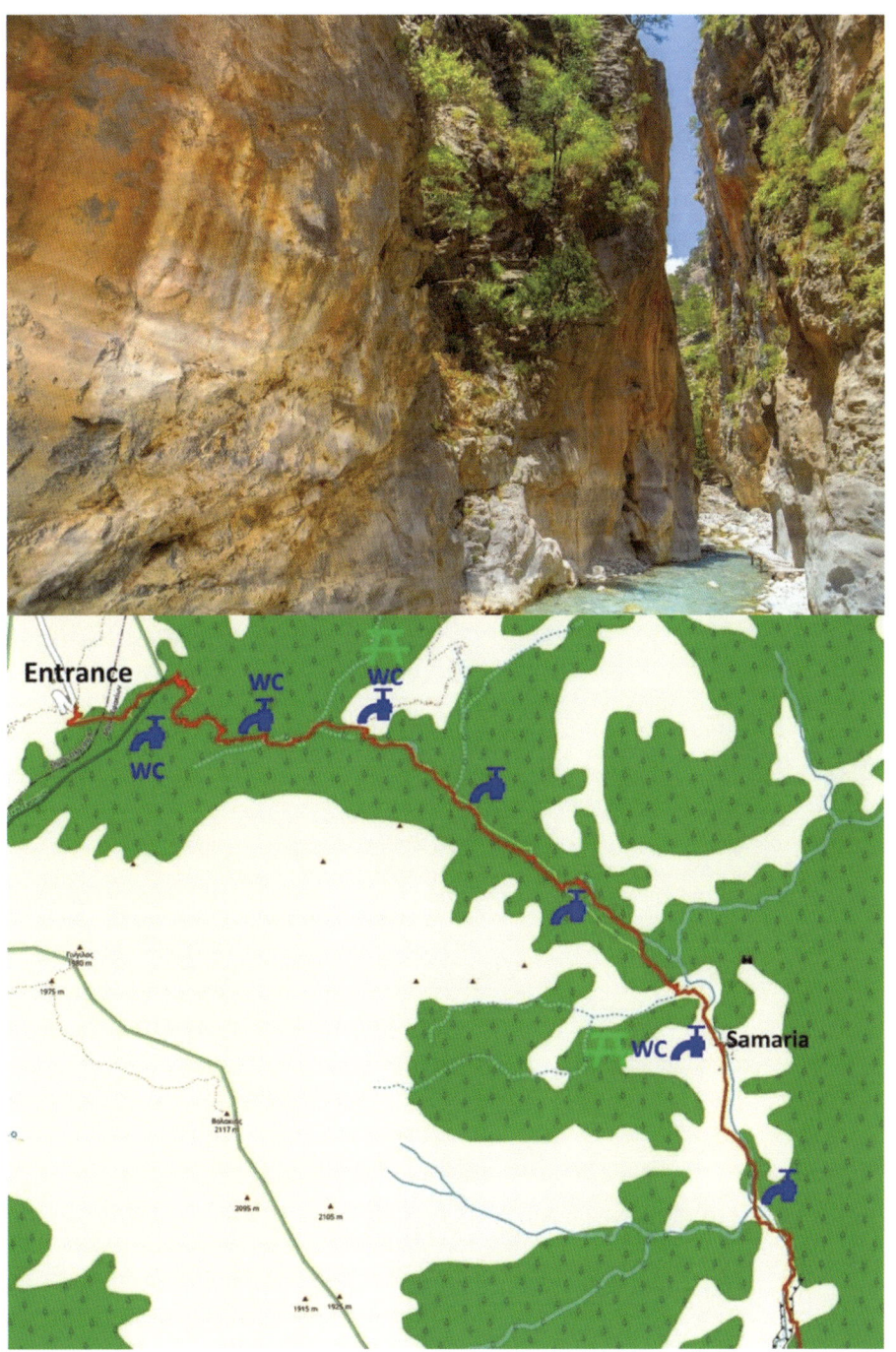

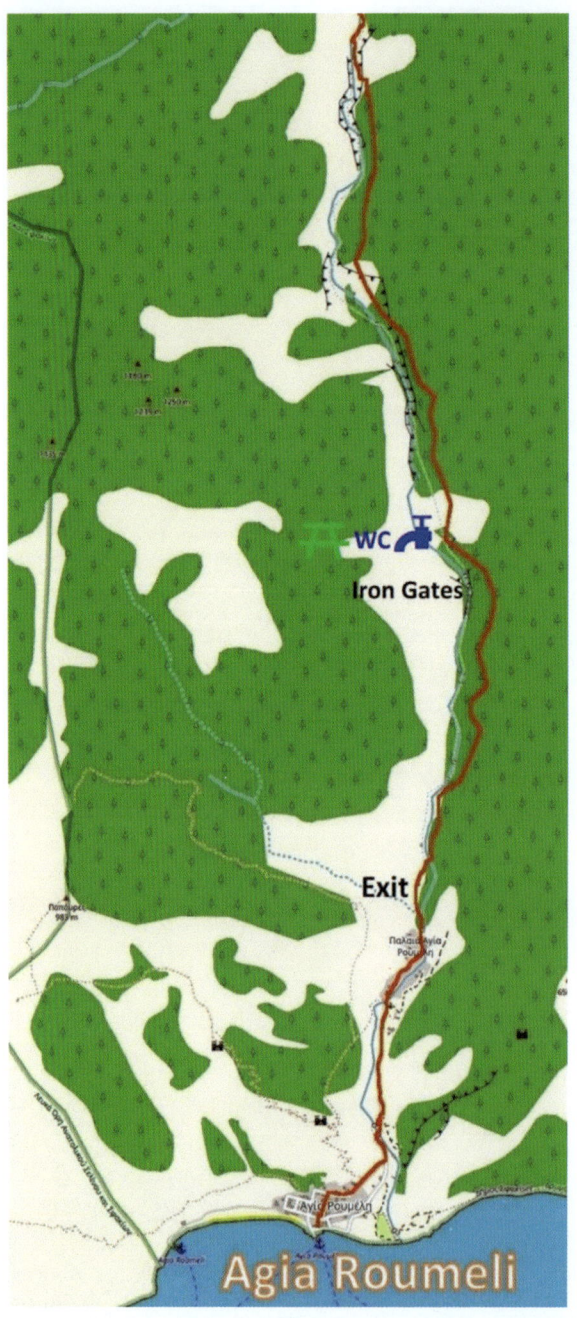

Cost:

There is a ticket office at the start, the cost in 2020 was Euro 5.00 (free to children under 15 and half price for students).

Opening Times:

The Gorge is open from May to October opening times are 07:00 to 15:00. From 15:00 visitors are only allowed to walk 2km into the gorge either from Xyloskalo at the top or from Agia Roumeli at the bottom.

Getting There:

The best way to arrive at the start at the top of the gorge is by bus from the bus station in Paleochora leaving early at 06:15 in the morning.

This means after your walk you can spend some time in Agia Roumeli (inaccessible by road) and take the ferry back. You can get joint bus and ferry tickets in Paleochora There are plenty of places to buy your ferry tickets in Agia Roumeli as well.

10. Errors, Omissions, Corrections

What is clear to me might not be clear to you on the ground following the directions in this book. It is my ambition that nobody is unable to follow the directions and maps to complete the walks. However things are constantly changing, new fences are put up or pulled down, fire breaks are bulldozed through where only narrow footpaths existed before, new signposts are erected or pulled down, paths become overgrown and olive farmers create new tracks. If you can help improve or update the information in this book, please do not hesitate to email me at Sam-J-Harris@Outlook.com .

11. Grading

The walks in this book are not graded as such because grading is very subjective depending on experience, fitness and expectations. There is one descriptor added to some of the walks and that is "Adventurous". These walks will involve routes where the path surface is loose and steep which may be above some people's ability. More detail is added to the description of the walks themselves. As a generalisation, it is possible to say that those who are able but new to walking should limit themselves to no more than 5 miles and 200m ascent. People who are used to walking should manage up to 8 miles and 600m ascent. Those that are fit and experienced will manage much more. If in doubt always start off with something that should be within your capability and build up to the harder walks. All this advice can be totally undermined by the ambient temperature. A six mile walk at 35 degC+ can be as exhausting as a 12 mile walk at 20 degC+. If not used to walking or out of practice or inexperienced with the high temperatures try smaller walks first, to gauge your ability, there are many short walks available in this book for this. Better to find it easy than overreach yourself and get into trouble.

12. Fence-Gates

Throughout the walks 'fence-gates' are mentioned. These are the most common form of 'gates' to be found in rural Crete. To explain, the fences are mainly made of wire latticed concrete reinforcement mesh wire, consisting of panels about 1.2m high and of various lengths. The fence posts are also made from concrete reinforcement rods. These must be incredibly cheap in Crete because they are everywhere. The panels are held together with twisted bailing wire. A fence-gate is a wire mesh panel where the twisted wires are easy to unravel on one side allowing passage through and resecuring by twisting the wire afterwards. Where there are paths and tracks the gates are always easy to open and often the 'hinge' side is created with loops of wire so that the gate doesn't need to bend to open. Sometimes there is no twisted wire, and the gate is held in place by interlacing the open ends of the mesh with the fence using the elasticity of the panel and friction to hold it in place. A little inspection and investigation will reveal the method to open the gate and resecure. For the control of livestock it is important to close gates, but also to leave open those that were found open. It is possible that they have been left this way to allow animals access to water or food. The general rule is to leave gates how you found them. I've heard of people claiming to carry small pairs of pliers to get through the fences in an emergency, this may be considered however, the need for this will only occur if you have lost the route and will not be taken kindly by the locals.

13. Maps

All maps in this book are **copywrite OpenStreetMap contributors,** one of which is the Author. I have added all the routes in this book to the maps using the GPS traces and arial photography so that they are available on apps and software using OSM. You may find the colours of the maps quite unnecessarily gaudy, a bit garish even. The reason for this is that the first time we took the printed copy out to check the directions we found we could not see the detail in the bright Cretan sunlight. This was particularly true for the standard format of white roads against a pale beige background. To help with this the colours have been enriched so that hopefully you will still be able to see the detail in the sunlight.

14. Ferries

There is no road along the southwest coast of Crete. Road routes are available between the main coastal destinations, but they involve driving up into the hills and back down again. An exception is Agia Roumeli at the end of the Samaria gorge which can only be reached by ferry and cannot be reached by road at all. The roads are narrow and incredibly circuitous with many tight hairpin bends.

They are littered with goats, fallen debris and rocks at random intervals, they are passable (the bus drivers manage with zen-like skills) but they are not quick. Fortunately, there are excellent ferries that hop along the coast allowing access to the coastal towns and opening up a host of walking opportunities and not least providing a good relaxing day out. There is one car ferry that goes east from Paleochora in the morning stopping along the way as far as Hora Sfakia and returns in the afternoon. There is also another foot only ferry that completes the same itinerary slightly out of sync by 15 minutes or so. There is also a ferry service to the island of Gavdos, but the other one that is relevant to this book is the one that is dedicated to taking passengers to and from Elephonisi beach west of Paleochora. Links to the ferry websites and timetables are at the end of the book.

Ferry warnings

This is Crete and things do not run as expected to the north European mind. Be advised that ferry timetables can vary daily or be cancelled due to changing weather conditions or the number of passengers or for whatever reason, so check the day before at the ticket offices around the ferry jetty for the latest intelligence in person; the latest information will not be on the web. Ask about the likelihood of the ferry being cancelled for both your outward and return journey.

If you read the small print on the car ferry ticket it says that you must be at the jetty 1 hour before departure which covers them for a multitude of sins. I was once left stranded in Sougia when the ferry left 10mins early, even though we could be seen clearly walking towards the ferry with only about 200m remaining on the road that only goes to the ferry

Ferry Routes

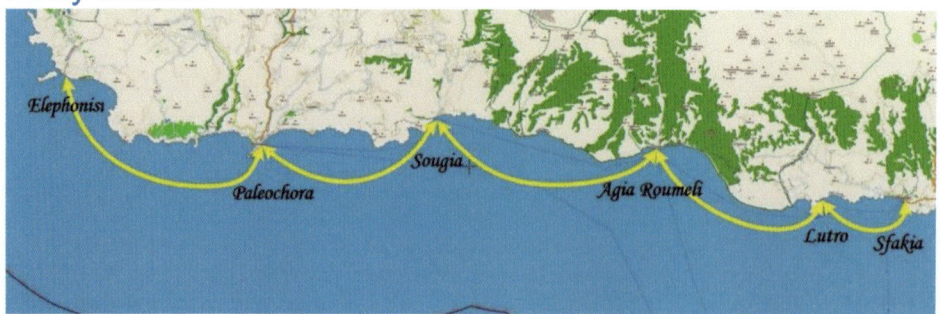

15. Useful Links

Depending on when you read this book these links may or may not be current but, a keyword search in your search engine of choice should be able to get you what you need.

Ferries

The car ferry company is Anendyk their web site is here: https://anendyk.gr/

The timetables can be found at https://anendyk.gr/?page_id=97

Bus

The Cretan bus company is E-KTEL you can find their timetables and book a ticket on the internet; their web site is here https://www.e-ktel.com/en/

Taxi

A local Paelochora company is Psarakis found at http://paleochora-taxi.com/

16. Satellite navigation, GPS and GPX

GPS stands for Global Positioning System which is a system for identifying location using satellite signals. When you record a route using a GPS system the file can be saved as a .gpx file. There are other formats, but GPX seems to be the most common. All routes in this book are available as GPX files for you to use with your smartphone or a dedicated handheld Sat Nav (if you must). To obtain the files email me at Sam-J-Harris@Outlook.com state your order number and that you would like the GPX files and I will happily send them all to you.

I highly recommend using a smartphone for GPS navigation. They are readily available, relatively inexpensive, have the same accuracy as any dedicated system and come with nice big screens, cameras, phones, the internet etc. etc.

There are many satellite navigation Apps available, to see the maps in this book you need one that uses Open Street Map (OSM) maps. Which app to use is quite a personal thing and many people use different ones to those mentioned here. I use Wikiloc, Mapsme and OsmAnd. Wikiloc is easy to use for recording routes, but you need to subscribe to follow a route. The GPX files can however be downloaded free using a PC and uploaded to use in another app or dedicated GPS device. Mapsme is particularly good and always seems to have the best up to date maps, but you can't upload or follow a route. OsmAnd is probably the best free app but has a complicated interface that takes some getting used to. Strava is very popular with runners and cyclists and has comprehensive facilities, but you need to subscribe to use it. Either way, apps are changing all the time and better choices could be available that are worth trying. On a slightly different matter on the Graphhopper website you can create and download your own gpx foot path routes.

17. Safety and Liability

The inclusion of walking routes and footpaths in this book does not mean that they are safe to use and negotiate. The Author does not accept liability for the safety of users of this book. At all times the reader is solely responsible for their own safety and for assessing the safety to undertake the walks in this book.

There are no public rights of way in Crete apart from the main European 'E' routes. It therefore follows, that the walks in this book not part of the European routes do not constitute any legal rights to use the routes and paths described by the walks. At all times be respectful of the environment, fences and gates, livestock, plants, trees, crops and property of the landowners. Always use existing paths and tracks and you shouldn't have any problems.

18. Walks Table in order of distance

Walk	Name	Distance		Ascent		Pg
		Miles	km	m	ft	
B	Paleochora Millstone Quarry	2.2	3.5	49	161	10
E	Vlithias	2.5	4.0	214	702	21
F	Azogires Monastery and Caves	2.8	4.5	305	1001	23
Q	Agia Roumeli Lower West Fort	2.8	4.4	291	955	56
G	Azogires Spaniakos Fort and the Cave of the 99 Holy Fathers	3.1	5.0	312	1023	25
A	Paleochora Town Tour	3.4	5.5	156	512	7
R	Sougia Circular	3.7	6.0	287	942	58
H	Krios, Three Beaches	4.5	7.2	332	1090	28
W	Agia Irini Gorge	4.7 or 9.0	7.5 or 14.5	-500	-1640	74
C	Paleochora Aerials	4.8	7.6	356	1168	12
K	Kandanos Churches and Ancient Tree	4.9 or 6.6	7.9 or 10.6	282 or 327	925 or 1071	36
D	Paleochora-Anidri	5.5	8.9	333 or 440	1093 or 1444	15
M	Milia	6.0	9.7	461	1512	42
I	Voutas to Karavopetra beach via the ridge tombs	6.2	10.0	194 -472	636 -1550	31
J	Voutas churches	6.4	10.3	452	1780	33
S	Sougia, Polyphemos Cave Adventurous	6.4	10.3	520	1703	60
L	Kandanos Southern Hills	6.7	10.8	441	1447	39
V	Elefonisi	7.0	11.3	257	843	71
N	Milia from Koutsomatados	7.3	11.7	655	2150	46
X	Samaria Gorge	9.3	15.0	-1250	-4101	76
T	Sougia, Polyphemos Cave	9.7	15.6	680	2231	63
O	Sarakina Valleys	9.9	14.4	520	1706	50
U	Sougia to Paleochora	10.2	16.4	554	1818	67
P	Topolia Gorge	10.7	17.2	696	2283	53

Printed in Great Britain
by Amazon